4 = 7-14-08

B.C.

Growing Into God

Meditations on the Two Great Commandments

Patricia Beall

Patricia Beall
Sanpan

Marshalls

Marshall Morgan and Scott
Marshall Pickering
3 Beggarwood Lane, Basingstoke, Hants RG23 7LP, UK

First published in 1986 by Marshall Morgan and Scott
Publications Ltd
Part of the Marshall Pickering Holdings Group
A subsidary of the Zondervan Corporation

All scripture quotations are from *The Jerusalem Bible* or *The
New Jerusalem Bible*, published by Darton, Longman and
Todd.

British Library Cataloguing in Publication Data
    Beall, Patricia
    Growing into God: Meditations on the two great
    commandments
    1. Lent—Meditations
    I. Title
    242'.34   BV85

ISBN 0-551-01319-2

Phototypeset in Linotron Plantin by
Input Typesetting Ltd, London
Printed in Great Britain by
Anchor Brendon Ltd, Tiptree Essex

Dedication

With love and appreciation for
Roland Walls, Uvedale Lambert, Graham Pulkingham

Three men of different age
yet all of the same era

Each
hearing and obeying
following and leading
into uncharted ways, unknown difficulties,
    unapplauded choices

Three faithful men
afraid and unafraid
obedient to the Spirit's call

Notes and Acknowledgements

Abram and Saul are also known by other names. Abram eventually became Abraham, for God re-named him; Saul, because his ministry was to the non-Jewish world, is famous as Paul, which is the Greek version. Throughout, however, I call them Abram and Saul, the names used in these scriptures which tell their stories.

It's also hard to know what to call God. I am convinced God is a person; and I don't believe God is only masculine. It is our language, not God, that is limited. But to preserve the warmth and truth of God's nature, namely, that it is personal, occasionally I use words like 'he', 'his', 'him', because they are common to our ear. I thought this the simplest solution to a difficult dilemma.

It's important to note some other names. Mel Lambert generously released her secretary, Val Holland, to type the manuscript; I am grateful to them both. I'm indebted as well to Alison Robbie, who also typed and proofread. Judy Powell and Dee Newnham, with their interest and prayer, were a graceful support. And special thanks to Bart Gavigan, whose razor intellect and gentle heart evaluated the manuscript. Additionally, he was always cheerful and encouraging, even when I wasn't.

Introduction

God's world is enormous. Our worlds are often tiny, limited by our experience, conditioned by our background, bounded by our needs and fears. But God's world is immense. His concerns are unlimited, his works are broad and far-reaching. It is we who are limited, we who make the world only as large as we want. We reduce God to a personal, local deity, meant to serve our city, protect our village, care for our church, favour our friends, meet the needs within our small circles.

Although God always grounds his word and work in local situations, God is not parochial. The works of the Spirit occur in specific locales, then reach out, spreading far and wide. The Spirit always goes forth, breaks through, goes beyond.

God's intent is the salvation and redemption of the whole world. All peoples, all cultures, all nations, are to share in the miracle of God's love. God works cross-culturally, making all things new in Christ, joining people in the body of Christ, empowering people to be a sign of the Kingdom.

I chose Jesus, Abram, Mary and Saul for this book because they were all part of new works that God wanted to accomplish. They all knew God, they all heard God, they all loved and served God. He asked for the whole of their lives, and they agreed. Each gave all, holding back nothing.

In these four, I see people who fulfilled, as best they

could, perhaps as perfectly as can be on earth, the greatest commandment there is, to *love the Lord your God with all your heart, with all your soul, with all your strength and with all your mind*.

I hope that their lives move and influence yours, as they have mine. Each of us is unique, a combination of strength and weakness, of gift and disability, of hope and despair. From the lives of these four wonderful people, we can see that the Holy Spirit is well able to redeem and use anything, if only we will offer it to God.

When you read this book, give a lot of time to the scriptures. They are more than just a starting point, more than a reference from which to make points. They are as important as the meditations. Read them carefully, re-read them frequently, dwelling on them.

Know God, hear God, love God, serve God. You will be joining Jesus and all the saints, you will be accompanied by the Holy Spirit, in accomplishing the works of God on earth.

Patricia Beall

South Park
Blechingley Surrey
November 1985

Contents

PART ONE:

JESUS KNOWS GOD
JOHN'S GOSPEL

Day 1

Jesus Knows God as Righteous

WHEN the time of the Jewish Passover was near Jesus went up to Jerusalem, and in the Temple he found people selling cattle and sheep and doves, and the money changers sitting there. (John 2:13–14)

Imagine the crowds in Jerusalem! Imagine thousands upon thousands of pilgrims from every corner of the country converging upon the capital.

See families, friends and animals, filling the rough roads, loaded with bedding, baggage, clothes, instruments, food, goods. See people spilling out of the inns, see them willing fields to empty, so tent cities can be raised.

See the Pharisees, meticulously attired and priding themselves on painstaking obedience to the Law. And the Sadducees, secure in their religious doctrine of after-life; and the Zealots, convinced the future of Judaism is in their restless hands. Watch the stall-keepers and money changers, the tradespeople, craftpeople and entertainers, the proprietors and servants. All are frantic with their wares, their work, their antics, their takings. This is high season, the most profitable time of the year!

Smell the rich heavy incense from the Temple, the sickly rawness of the slaughterhouses, the sweat and garbage of the streets. Inhale the smoke from the braziers, the stench of the leather tanners, the throttling musk of the goats. The appeal of sweetmeats and the tang of spices are mixed with the bitterness of drying dung, blood, sour milk.

Look again at the crush of ordinary people. They stream into the streets, herd to the gardens and Temple, throng the marketplace in fear and abandon. They are elated, staggered, culture shocked by the city's colours, size and unfamiliarity.

What matter that the sacrificial animals must be bought at outrageous prices? What matter that the Temple exchange rate is literally extortionate? After all, this is Jerusalem! Days are long and hot and bright, nights cool and filled with wine, storytelling and laughter. The offerings, once given, can be forgotten: the barter, the gossip, the thrilling sights of the Queen of Cities make up for lesser things. One shows to distant relatives the sons grown strong and the beautiful daughters; one delights in the happy acquisition of a healthy goat or sturdy donkey; one makes a pleased display of plentiful, brightly-coloured, new-woven blankets, symbol of the success of the season's sheep shearing. What matter anything! One only lives once, and Passover comes only once a year . . .

What matter, indeed. Jesus' discernment was acute and penetrating as he surveyed the pilgrims. He saw that the structural degeneration of the Temple system was matched by a popular decay. It was not only systemic corruption that agitated Jesus, it was the personal corruption in his people's hearts. After all, markets don't exist in a vacuum! There must be buyers as well as sellers, trading isn't without two parties, bartering is not one-sided! The people did not challenge their oppression. Instead, they colluded with it. It served them, too.

12

Worshippers at the festival had forgotten that God was the source and point and purpose of their lives. Jesus saw that the pilgrims' good times, their new blankets and camels, their pride in their families, were the real treasures of their hearts. Rather than offering themselves to God, they offered substitutes. Rather than giving the whole of their lives to God – their thoughts, words, relationships, activities, personal economies, actions – the people gave only the prescribed sacrifices, birds, animals and coins. They attended the services, said the words and sang the songs. They gave what the Law required.

But what does God require?

It is sacrifice of the *heart*. It is kindness and fairness in everyday life, mercy and compassion in spirit and action. It is humility towards God. Religious attendance is not good enough, ritual observance not good enough, required sacrifices not good enough. They are symbol, not substance!

And God, as righteous, will not be mocked. Jesus knew God's abhorrence of infidelity. God despises lip-service which lacks a soft heart, outward obedience which shields inward selfishness, a nod in the direction of God while one's heart is self-seeking.

Jesus saw in the precinct in Jerusalem what he later rejected in the church at Laodicea: 'I know about your activities: how you are neither cold nor hot. I wish you were one or the other, but since you are neither hot nor cold, but only lukewarm, I will spit you out of my mouth. You say to yourself, I am rich, I have made a fortune and have everything I want, never realising that you are wretchedly and pitiably poor, and blind and naked too. I warn you, buy from me the gold that has been tested in the fire to make you truly rich, and white robes to clothe you and hide your shameful nakedness, and eye ointment to put on your eyes to enable you to see. I reprove and train those whom I love: so repent in real earnest.' (Rev. 3:15–19)

Jesus' stripping of the Temple courts was a judgement on the whole religious culture of his people. The worshippers at the national festival in Jerusalem didn't manifest God's characteristics of fidelity, justice, mercy and humility; and Jesus let them know it.

God has not changed. The Spirit still burns with fiery indignation and fierce fury when God's people fail to worship with the whole of their lives. God's righteousness is the standard which will judge us. Do you eat while others starve, do you buy more clothes while others are still naked, do you fill your home with goods while others haven't even a house? Our attendance at church and our lists of good works will not save us. We will be found righteous through obedience to Christ, by fulfilling the law of love, in living out the spirit and not the letter of God's laws.

Prayer

Lord,

I worship you as Saviour. You have sought me, loved me, redeemed me. You bought me with your blood, freeing me to receive God's love.

Help me to worship whole-heartedly. Show me by your Spirit the times and ways in my daily life when I devalue the price you paid for me. Let me see my indulgence and my selfishness, so that I can repent in real earnest. Please reprove and train me, so that my life and actions reflect yours. Amen.

Practice

Consider your last five purchases. Were all necessary or were some extravagant? Instead of buying, could you have shared with others?

Day 2

Jesus Knows God as Parent

---

*MAKING a whip out of cord, he drove them all out of the Temple, sheep and cattle as well, scattered the money changers' coins, knocked their tables over and said to the dove-sellers, 'Take all this out of here and stop using **my Father's house** as a market'. Then his disciples remembered the words of scripture: I am eaten up with zeal for your house. (John 2:15–17)*

In the havoc of the upturned market, in the midst of preparations for the most important national festival of the year, Jesus for the first time in John's gospel speaks publicly about his relationship to God.

'Stop using *my Father's* house as a market.'

With two words, Jesus identifies himself as intimate with God. All Jews were creatures of God and servants of God, but Jesus goes much further. He announces he is a *child* of God. By virtue of his maleness, the *son* of God.

Which was most shocking for the Jews that day? The fact that with whip and word, Jesus demolished the accepted system for giving to God, or the fact that he made an unprecedented, impassioned, public statement about his personal relationship to God?

There is no doubt that Jesus' meaning was instantly comprehended. Everyone knew *exactly* what Jesus meant. In the Jewish culture, family relationships were vital and clearly understood. Sons were preferred: every man hoped to have not just one but many sons. Fathers gave their sons everything, shared their lives completely with their heirs; the sons, in turn, became fathers and passed on the life and inheritance they had received. So did the Jew live forever, in the generations to come.

Jesus' statement was scandalous to his hearers precisely because it *was* understood. And understood perfectly, as perfect blasphemy. No one – *no one* – could claim God as parent rather than creator, as Father rather than source. As far as the Jews were concerned, God had already been revealed as fully as possible on earth, to their forefathers. Further revelation, especially in terms of intimacy, was neither expected nor acceptable. *No one*, of that tradition and culture, could say they were a child of God.

But Jesus did, one weekday afternoon as he strode through the Temple precinct, acting, for all the world to see, 'as if he owned the place.'

As indeed, in Jesus' terms, he did. And this is his second overt offence. To *speak* blasphemy was the first, but to *enact* it crowned the sin. This proved the heights of arrogance deceiving the young man.

Jesus' actions show how seriously he took his relationship as God's son. Any son or daughter who inherits from their parents receives not only the property, but also the responsibility of it. Just so with Jesus. Knowing the Temple was his Father's house, he accepted responsibility for it. In this case, responsibility was two-fold. First, the action of casting out; second, the statement of ownership which explained his action.

This unity of work and word in his relationship to God is seen over and again in Jesus' life. Jesus knew God was his parent, Jesus knew he was the son of his Father. He stunned people, shocked people, offended people, because he refused to make into an abstraction the intimacy and depth of his personal relationship with God.

This relationship to God as parent was not theoretical or spiritualised. Jesus was not philosophical about it, using it as an analogy for teaching or to make examples. Nor was he ethereal about it, removing the relationship from the realm of bricks and mortar, animals and birds, money and people. Rather, Jesus was *incarnate* in it. He insisted on grounding his sonship to his Father on the earth, in the same terms, the same ways, that people live their daily lives: parent and child, father and son, inheritance and heir, property and responsibility.

It was this groundedness, this earthiness, this earthliness, this reality of heaven made flesh on earth, this *incarnation*, that caused Jesus to be feared, despised, attacked and arrested. And eventually, got rid of.

Could you be found guilty of this same 'blasphemy'?

Prayer

Jesus,

Lead me ever more surely, ever more clearly, ever more certainly, along the way you go.

Help me discover the God who is parent and father, the God you love, the God you know. Amen.

Practice

Look around your area, and find one of the 'no man's lands', such as an area of wasteground, greens littered with rubbish, river banks scattered with debris. Gather your family, neighbours or friends, and work together for a morning, restoring this tiny bit of God's creation.

Day 3

Jesus Knows God as Homemaker

'*TAKE all of this out of here and stop using my Father's house as a market.*' (*John 2:16*)

We can often be found in our houses.

Not necessarily our physical presence, but our personality, our characteristics, our style. It's rare, when visiting someone's home for the first time, that we are surprised by what we find. Rather, the colours, the decoration, the contents, usually bear out what we already know. When this isn't the case, we learn a lot very quickly about the person we thought we knew! Because houses represent those who dwell there.

Whether we rent or buy a house, we live in it as if we own it. In our homes we speak our most caring words and share our most private thoughts, in them we reveal ourselves most personally, we are most abandoned in intimacy or anger. Houses, in our time as in Jesus', are personal centres.

Markets, in our time as in Jesus', are conglomerate centres. Markets are full of bargaining, bustle, competition, noise, hustle, rush, stimulation, skill, cleverness, time pressure, threat of loss. Markets are a constant bass-drum beat of anxiety and necessity, whether real or contrived.

Stock markets shake with clacking machines, ringing telephones, flurrying people, flashing screens, all crying the pace at which the economic world hurtles. Street markets are jumbled stalls, draped with fabric, clothes, goods, vegetables, meat, displayed provocatively, signalling what we mustn't miss. Eastern markets are a huddle, a splash and a stretch of booths, bazaars, stalls, tables, with people careering carelessly, snatching up goods to place in your face, reaching out, with voice and hand, to attract your entire attention. Children, carts, buggies, animals, motorbikes, men, women – all clatter in cacophony, touching, hustling, hurrying, sure of your necessities.

Houses are not bazaars, homes are not markets. We don't expect them to be. Nor did Jesus expect to find his Father's house a market. His expectation had been quite different.

In the Temple, Jesus expected to find the personal characteristics of the owner. The Temple was God's house, the sign and symbol of God's dwelling with humankind. So in his Father's house, Jesus expected to experience his Father's personality. There would be God's love, God's mercy, God's tenderness, God's compassion. There would be proclamation of God's word, and its faithful fulfillment. These signs would blaze from God's house, a glorious testimony to the Lord of all creation who welcomes everyone, who makes a home for every person and creature.

For Jesus knows God as a homemaker. God gathers up the broken, comforts the afflicted, cares for the neglected, welcomes the wanderer. God washes the feet of the weary, restores the souls of the wounded, heals the bodies of the diseased, eases the lonely.

Jesus knows God as a homemaker, as the one who has opened heaven and heart to give, receive and share. Jesus knows God as the one who gives a home to the oppressed, the one who promises and provides a place of safety and security for the dispossessed. This home-making God is a family person, reaching out to all who will respond, drawing in all who will enter. And what did Jesus find in the Temple? Powerful characteristics indeed, but not of his God.

He found traders and stall-holders, selling animals and birds to the pilgrims for Temple sacrifices. But their prices were **exorbitant**, grossly unfair. The prices were highly inflated, because the traders had a monopoly on required goods.

Jesus found money-changers, exchanging regional currency for the coinage required for Temple offerings. But the rates were exaggerated, grossly unfair. The exchange rates were highly inflated because the money-changers possessed what others needed.

He found a Temple hierarchy and staff that not only encouraged but legalised this corruption. *Only* those creatures purchased from the Temple sellers could be used: no other sacrifices were accepted. *Only* that currency purchased from the Temple money-changers could be used: no other coinage was allowed.

Further, Jesus found this market established in the part of the Temple used by those who sought God but weren't Jews. Certainly this added insult to injury! Gentiles, pagans and proselytes, seeking God, had been displaced, put out of the one area where they could worship.

What did Jesus find at his Father's house? In short, a market in all of its worst aspects. Greed, extortion, manipulation, usury, hard-heartedness. Personal gain at the expense of the poor, use of the property for barter, not worship. He found, allied to religion, an economic system which thrived on depriving the faithful and rejecting the outcasts. He did not find love, mercy, tenderness, compassion.

So his cord became a whip, his words a scourge, his outrage an energising force. His love was exercised, his mercy and tenderness were stirred, his compassion burst into flame. The fire of his heart and eyes and voice consumed the sin around him, his passion for his Father and his house devoured the corruption surrounding him.

' "Take all this out of here and stop using my Father's house as a market!" Then his disciples remembered the words of scripture: *I am eaten up with zeal for your house.*'

20

Prayer

Lord,
 Fill my life with zeal for God and God's purposes.

 Take this temple of flesh, my body, in which you dwell by the Spirit, and cleanse it further. Renew in me the power of love, enlarge mercy and tenderness, broaden and deepen compassion.

 Do all this for your sake, as well as my own. Amen.

Practice

Look again at your church or place of worship. Does it represent God? Plan two things you and others could do to show whose house it is.

Day 4

Jesus Knows God as Satisfier

*J*ESUS *came to Jacob's well and, tired by the journey, sat straight down. It was just about noonday. When a Samaritan woman came to draw water, Jesus said to her, 'Give me a drink.' His disciples had gone into the town to buy food. The Samaritan woman said to him, 'What? You are a Jew and you ask me, a Samaritan, for a drink?' – Jews, of course, do not associate with Samaritans.*

Jesus replied: 'If you only knew what God is offering and who it is saying to you: "Give me a drink", you would have been the one to ask, and he would have given you living water'.

'You have no bucket, sir,' she answered, 'and the well is deep: how could you get this living water? . . .'

Jesus replied: 'Whoever drinks this water will get thirsty again; but no one who drinks the water that I shall give will ever be thirsty again: the water that I shall give will turn into a spring inside him, welling up to eternal life'.

'Sir', said the woman 'give me some of that water so that I may never get thirsty and never have to come here again to draw water'. (John 4:5–11, 13–15)

Take a moment, and recall the time in your life when you suffered terribly, most terribly, from thirst.

Think back, to when you were hot as you had never been hot. You were exhausted, utterly worn out from heat; you were parched, utterly thirsty.

Where were you? Was your area plagued suddenly by a freakishly hot streak, or were you travelling? Was the heat thick and moist, filled with unreleased water, or was it a sultry dry heat, sapping your skin, nose and mouth of their last reserves of moisture? Were you in a desert? Was it a barren place, of wind and dune and shuffled, bleached rocks, or did it have spindly shrubs, flat floors, distant hills?

Think back, until you remember when it was, what you thought and perhaps even feared. Could you change your circumstance, or did time belong to someone else: a tour driver, a water repair board, an emergency auto service? Were you sure your situation *would* change? Were you sure you'd be rescued from nature's power?

The distance Jesus and his friends were walking, from Judea near Jerusalem to Galilee, was about fifty miles. The well at Sychar was about half way. We read that when they arrived, 'Jesus, tired by the journey, sat straight down.' And no wonder. It was the heat of the day and stiflingly hot, they would been walking since the cool of dawn, it was lunchtime and they had no food. At least there was a well, where thirst could be quenched.

But without a bucket, Jesus couldn't draw. So he waited until a local came by, then, without even saying 'please', told the stranger to give him water.

Seemingly, she demurred. She was shocked, perhaps a bit put off, and probably thirsty herself. So there they were: a man and a woman, a stranger and a local, an Israelite and a Samaritan. Both at the same well, both talking, both thirsty.

But Jesus' thirst was different from the woman's. Water would remove his. Then, when thirsty again, he would drink again. The thirst he saw in her, however, was not temporary. It was not caused by heat, desert or empty winds. It was a thirst of nature, not of creatureliness.

It was the thirst of a soul for love, for acceptance, for understanding, for meaning. It was the thirst of a body for tenderness, for passion, for exchange and appreciation. It was the thirst of a quick-witted, theological mind for truths that would not waver with debate, for philosophy that would not pander to nationalism, for teaching that would not teeter by intimidation. And it was the thirst of a spirit for that succour, that refreshment, that living water, that would never cease.

No, this woman's thirst was not temporary, or even temporal. It came from God, and only God could relieve it. The thirst was total: it was the intense longing of the whole human creature, to know and be known, to love and be loved, to satisfy and be satisfied.

Jesus recognised this thirst. He recognised it in others because he had not turned away from it in himself. Jesus was not a stranger to such seeking. He knew the intensity of our human capacity to desire and love, yet how vulnerable we are because of it. Jesus also knew, as this woman did not, that God could satisfy her.

For he himself was satisfied. He had drunk of God's water and knew, from the fullness within his soul and the well-spring of his body, from the depth of knowledge in his mind and the peace in his spirit, that God was satisfying. He himself was satisfied. In God he found refreshment, enabling, encouragement. With God he experienced friendship, acceptance, appreciation. Through God he loved others and was loved by them, knew others and was enjoyed by them.

Yes, Jesus recognised this thirst. He knew it was as unlike his own thirst as the beating mid-day sun was unlike the still mid-night moon that would come later. He thirsted because he walked; she thirsted because she wandered. He thirsted because he was tired; she thirsted because she was tired. He thirsted from exertion and talking, she thirsted from exhaustion and tears, from hopeless affairs and heightened despair, from satiation which was never satisfying.

Yes, Jesus recognised this woman's thirst. He knew that water from God would absorb it, drown it, flood it. Pure water, healing water, clear water, 'living' water. God's heavenly water, satisfaction on earth.

'If you only knew what God is offering,' Jesus tells us, 'you would ask and God would give you living water.'

Prayer

Lord,

I offer you the thirst of my loneliness, the bitterness of my fear, the dryness of my soul's natural springs.

Accept, receive, relieve, so your Spirit's living water will well up from within, satisfying me, refreshing others. Amen.

Practice

Recall something you've been asked to do, but have avoided or neglected. Do it.

Day 5

Jesus Knows God as Sustainer

---

*M*EANWHILE, *the disciples were urging him,
'Rabbi, do have something to eat'; but he said, 'I
have food to eat that you do not know about'. So the
disciples said to one another, 'Has someone brought him
food?'*

*But Jesus said: 'My food is to do the will of the one who
sent me, and to complete his work.'* (*John 4:31–34*)

Really, the disciples hadn't been gone all that long.
They'd gone straight into town, bought bread and probably wine, cheese and maybe some dates or figs, and
come directly back. Surely they were pleased with themselves, proud that Jesus had rested while they'd shopped,
proud they'd got the lunch so quickly and easily in a
semi-foreign country. Perhaps they hoped to be com-
mended for their care, congratulated on their effi-
ciency.

You can almost see their flourish of pleasure and
magnitude: *Rabbi, do have something to eat*. What an
instant deflation, what a strong flashing disappointment,
when Jesus refused.

And what a confusion, too! *Other* food? Where could
he have got it from? Who could have given him
anything? No one was around except this Samaritan
woman, and all she had were the waterjugs. Jesus
couldn't have sent someone else, they would have passed
them on the road. Nor did Jesus *look* as if he'd eaten.
No basket, no crumbs, no fruit stones cast aside or fish
bones collected in a neat stack. What was going on?

As often happened, the disciples spoke to each other,

not Jesus. *Has someone brought him food?* And, as usual, Jesus intervened, answering what was unasked. *My food is to do the will of the one who sent me, and to complete his work*. But, and again as usual, Jesus' explanation only increased their lack of understanding. What *was* he talking about?

First, we must realise that when Jesus speaks, his meaning is direct and literal. If not, he lets us know. He says, The Kingdom of God is *like* or *Suppose* one of you or *Once there was* a woman. Then we know it's a story or parable or example. Otherwise, Jesus makes straightforward statements to be taken at face value.

So when he says, 'My food is to do the will of the one who sent me, and to complete his work', he means just that. And probably like the disciples, we still don't understand.

Consider the meaning of the main word. What does *food* really mean?

Food is a necessity. Without it we literally perish. Humans require food, they cannot exist without it. This must not be ignored or made romantic. Picture again the victims and refugees of the great African famines of our age. They prove our life-and-death dependence upon food. Food sustains us.

Food is a stimulant, it is pleasurable. Foods vary, in colour, texture and taste; some we adore, others we abhor. Rarely, do we who have the luxury of choosing our food, eat what we don't like. We reject what we don't prefer, we placate cooks or consciences with a 'no-thank you' serving. We enjoy food, we enjoy what it does to us, we enjoy how we feel after eating it.

Food is a symbol, of friendship, entertainment, celebration. We invite our dearest friends or relatives for a meal, and prepare special foods we know they like. We invite important guests or business associates, and prepare costly or unusual foods, hoping to impress and satisfy them.

In doing these things, we take a risk. For eating is

actually an intimate act. Consuming food means opening ourselves, taking something in. Eating with others makes us vulnerable and exposed because we're willing to be seen adding something to ourselves. We're willing to have witnesses as we perform an act of survival and pleasure.

Inviting people to our homes, or out for a meal, is also risky. Our offerings may be rejected, if people dislike what we've provided or think it isn't good enough.

Food then, is no small matter. Our lives revolve around it, physically, emotionally, professionally, spiritually. And Jesus, speaking about food, is speaking simply and unadornedly about his relationship with God. He declares that in fulfilling God's will and finishing God's work, he is sustained. He is fed, filled, strengthened, pleasured, befriended, nourished. His physical needs are met, his emotional and spiritual needs are filled, his 'professional' requirements are satisfied.

In doing God's will – in his everyday actions of speaking, teaching, touching, healing, challenging, encountering, releasing, ordering, renewing – Jesus is sustained and nourished.

In completing the work God has begun – in dwelling in flesh on the earth, in revealing the Word of God and the power of the Spirit, in enlivening creation with the incarnate presence of its creator – Jesus is made healthy, finds joy and friendship, experiences intimacy and vulnerability, discovers variety, stimulation and satisfaction.

Can this be so? Can a relationship with God be so real, so tangible, so physical, that it is food to our humanity?

Yes, it can; and Jesus is the living testimony.

Prayer

God of all life,
I would like to know your will well, and be steadfast in completing your work.

Fill me with your love, so I can share with others. Feed me with your mercy, so I can care for others. Nourish me with your truth, so I can give honestly to others.

Sustain me by your Spirit, so I learn to trust you for all I need.

Amen.

Practice

Eat lightly for one day, having bread for breakfast, soup or fruit for your other meals. Put aside 15–30 minutes for quiet and prayer.

Day 6

Jesus Knows God as Challenger

*H*E *went again to Cana in Galilee, where he had changed the water into wine. Now there was a court official there whose son was ill at Capernaum and, hearing that Jesus had arrived in Galilee from Judea, he went and asked him to come and cure his son as he was at the point of death. Jesus said, 'So you will not believe unless you see signs and portents!' 'Sir,' answered the official 'come down before my child dies.' 'Go home,' said Jesus 'your son will live.' (John 4:46–49)*

When children are entrusted to us for twenty-four hours a day, twelve months a year, fifteen or eighteen or forty years running, depending on the capacity of the child, feelings which were unforeseen and unpredictable erupt.

When blood streams from our child's forehead, when our child's stomach is pumped from an overdose of pills, when our child has an untameable fever or a debilitating, untreatable disease, we feel very differently than when it's the child of someone down the road, or a co-worker or even a friend. When our child has a confusion of sight and mind that makes reading impossible, or a conjunction of emotion and reality that make the isolation of autism more secure that the world as we know it – when these things happen, we find unleashed responses more complex, more painful, more chaotic, than we ever would have thought possible.

There are many reasons why. It is literally our own 'flesh and blood' which is vulnerable. This child is *us*, extended into the present and projected into the future. Life as we expect it is challenged: boundaries and barriers suddenly erected. We are at the mercy of fate, or happenstance, or medicine, or God.

So with the court official working in Cana, twenty miles from Capernaum where his son was dying.

Responsibility was strongly developed in this man. He was a nobleman, with cares for property, lands and people. He was a court official, with political commitments and a regularised schedule. He was married with at least one child, which meant providing for his family.

He was also familiar with exercising power. His servants and tenants obeyed him, his staff at the court was trained to achieve his goals. This was a man accustomed to discipline, obedience, attention and action.

He was also loving and caring. Although working during this family crisis, he was not so immersed that he forgot his fears and hopes for his child. No sooner had Jesus arrived than he went to him, requesting his son's health.

Read the scripture again, and notice Jesus' response.

What a time for a challenge! This was a *very* important person, a very official, well-placed, responsible, powerful person. This event was a personal and regional crisis! Why was Jesus being so difficult?

He wasn't. Jesus knew that God is asked for many things for many reasons, and he wanted to know the nobleman's real motives. Was this a test question, part of the religious establishment's dossier on whether or not Jesus performed enough 'signs' to qualify him as a true prophet? Was this a cultural challenge, testing whether the God and prophet of the Jews would be kind to foreign national pagans who kept Rome's peace? Was this a plea of faith and doubt, with the person pitting his faith in God against what he wanted God to do for him?

Jesus met this man straight on, going to the heart of the matter. He challenged him, point blank.

Jesus couldn't have done this if he weren't used to

31

being challenged, by God and man. While challenge is often threatening, it is also a tool for clarification. When we must go to the heart of a matter, and do, we often discover, to our surprise and relief, that our position is valid, our intentions are true, our ambitions are not selfish or our hopes false.

Jesus, in his relationship of prayer, action and supplication with God, was constantly challenged. Jesus, in his work, his travelling ministry of teaching, healing, questioning, restoring, was constantly challenged.

These challenges were not unfortunate, although they were demanding and wearing. But through them Jesus matured in his relationship with God and became more capable in his relationships with people. Because God was direct with Jesus, Jesus was able to be direct with others. And it was always for the good, proving what motives, manipulations, ambivalences were really there. Challenge, from God to Jesus and from Jesus to others, was a positive, purifying dynamic. Deceptions surfaced, motives came clean, understanding was deepened.

We may not like Jesus' challenge to the nobleman, but he himself had no problem with it. He didn't sway, he didn't hesitate, he didn't stutter anxiously at Jesus' blunt interrogation. We don't know why. Perhaps because his heart was absolutely pure. Perhaps, because he was plunged into the agonising uncertainties of a responsible parent gone helpless, because he was entirely at the mercy of his hope of healing from God, he didn't even take in the nature of Jesus' challenge. Perhaps he instinctively went to the heart of the matter for himself, which was 'Sir, come down before my child dies!' Don't debate, don't ask questions which cloud the issue, don't load up this crisis with concerns which aren't mine. Please, just cure my child, save my son!

Jesus did. He didn't even go to Capernaum, he gave him the desire of his heart there and then. Jesus had tested this man, and not find him wanting; Jesus challenged him, and found him equal to the penetration.

Prayer

Lord,
 I don't want to be afraid of you. I don't want to fear your questions, your challenges.
 I want you to be able to examine my life closely – my motives, my reasons, my actions, my activities.
 Continue to open your life to me, Jesus, so I can see how you and God relate to each other. Speak to me through the scriptures, so I can see clearly the similarities between the things I face and the things you faced. Amen.

Practice

Visit a child who is confined to hospital. Pray for them at home after each visit. If you're housebound, ask a friend to give you a photo of a sick child they know. Pray for the child regularly.

Day 7

Jesus Knows God as Healer

---

*N*OW *at the Sheep Pool in Jerusalem there is a*
building, called Bethesda in Hebrew, which means
house of mercy. It consists of five porticos; and under these
were crowds of sick people – blind, lame, paralysed – waiting
for the water to move; for at intervals the angel of the Lord
came down into the pool, and the water was disturbed,
and the first person to enter the water after this disturbance
was cured of any ailment he suffered from. One man there
had an illness which had lasted thirty-eight years, and when
Jesus saw him lying there and knew he had been in this
condition for a long time, he said, 'Do you want to be well
again?' 'Sir,' replied the sick man 'I have no one to put
me into the pool when the water is disturbed; and while I
am still on the way, someone else gets there before me.'
Jesus said, 'Get up, pick up your sleeping-mat and walk'.
The man was cured at once, and he picked up his mat
and walked away. (John 5:2–9)

This description of Bethesda conjures up an image of
Victorian Bedlams.

In those large, multi-storied houses, hundreds of sick
people were incarcerated. Damaged and helpless,
suffering from every kind of illness and disease, people
were grouped almost at random. Some were chained,
others caged, others confined permanently to 'beds'
which were pallets of rags or straw. Emotional illness,
spiritual bondage and sickness, hideous physical disabilities, distortions resulting from the inept surgery of the
times – all types of deprivation were treated as depravity,
and jumbled together.

Treatment was infrequent and even then often inhumane. Agonies of violence and even malevolence were released upon the 'patients'. Wardens were glorified guards, social jailers. Parenting boards frequently regarded the 'inmates' not as humans but as fodder for the social and medical mills of experimentation and curiosity. Attendants were not trained or qualified, and very little 'attending' ever happened.

Visitors genuinely concerned for the sick were rare, but sight-seeing parties were common, Sunday afternoon excursions to goggle and gape at 'unfortunates', the 'creatures'. Occasionally a truly concerned doctor or relative tried to improve some individual's situation; on the whole, few rays of light pierced the shroud of Victorian ignorance, fear and intolerance.

Bethesda was the same. A concentrated centre of human misery, a random mixing of the damaged and helpless. Under the five porticos blind lay next to lame, lame barred the way of the paralysed, paralysed couldn't get to the healing waters because they had no help. And the emotionally crippled and spiritually oppressed were there too, double victims of illness.

As at Bedlam, there was no sophisticated or even sanitary treatment. Contagious coughs, infested bedding, filthy unwashed clothes, remnants of food and collections of garbage: disease passed from person to person. Illnesses inevitably became more complicated because of the lack of care, medicine, treatment.

Impotent is the word used in the King James version to describe Bethesda's captives: . . . a great multitude of impotent folk, of blind, halt, withered . . .'. It summarises excellently. The peoples' illnesses made them dependent, this dependency created impotence, the impotence bred despair.

Hear the response of the man who had been at Bethesda for *thirty-eight* years. When Jesus asked, 'Do you want to get well again?', the man didn't even answer the question. He just listed the reasons why health was impossible. 'I have no one to help me', 'When I try, someone gets there first'. He had been there the length of two generations already, he had lived in his illness for years, he had no other home. He had given up entirely. He was utterly impotent, chronically despairing.

Jesus didn't question him further. Jesus assumed the man's desire for health: and granted it.

But see how he did it. The words of healing were spoken as a command. They demanded that the man himself participate. This was no passive healing: the sufferer must be active in accomplishing it.

'Get up, pick up your sleeping-mat and walk.' This was a three-fold imperative, and it made the impotent cripple a partner in grace with God. Move, make the effort, Jesus required. Accept responsibility for your possessions, carry them, take charge of that which you own. Step out, propel yourself, move forward, enter into life. And the man did.

Jesus hadn't questioned further because he'd seen that two keys were needed to release this man from his personal prison of impotence and illness. First, the man had to know that change was possible; second, he had to know how it could happen.

Jesus' command, simple and short, showed him both. But it was not a passive grace which was bestowed. It was an active, demanding, strengthening grace, requiring the complete involvement of its recipient. The man had to make every effort. Healing couldn't have occurred if he had been content to remain helpless and dependent. Restoration to a full life was possible only if the word of God was obeyed as well as heard.

How must you move, for God's fullness to fill your life? What must you pick up, what responsibilities do you avoid, because they are too great or you are too fearful? What forward movement would change your life, releasing you from impotence of thought, deed or relationship?

Reflect on the questions above. Then speak with God,

and listen for answers, now and in the days to come. Because the healing word of God always contains two things: the fact that change is possible, and how it can happen.

Prayer

Lord,

I want to leave my Bethesdas. I want to get up, to change the situations in my life where I am dependent, impotent, despairing. Help me admit them, help me change them by listening carefully to you.

At the same time, prevent me from rushing. Sometimes I am so eager to please you, or so frightened of not obeying you, that I don't go carefully enough. Steady me as I move, so the solutions to my problems will be sound, not produced by my panic. I want to leave my Bedlams, too, Lord. In your Name, Jesus, Amen.

Practice

Contribute money or time to a group that works with the disabled or mentally handicapped.

Day 8

Jesus Knows God as Teacher

WHEN the feast of Tabernacles was half over, Jesus went to the Temple and began to teach. The Jews were astonished and said, 'How did he learn to read? He has not been taught.' Jesus answered them, 'My teaching is not from myself: it comes from the one who sent me.'
(*John 7:14–16*)

It was no small matter for Jesus to read in a synagogue or teach at a national festival.

The Jews were not a literate culture. In origin they were a tribal people, for many generations they were a nomadic people, finally they became an agrarian people. They were highly knowledgeable, well-versed and fluent in their history, laws and religion. But this was due to the strength of their oral tradition, not to common literacy.

This oral tradition passed Jewish culture from one generation to the next in many ways. There was story-telling, dramatic ritual, regular re-enactment of historic events. People said the commandments over and over, praise and religious responses were constant and on-going. At home, in the synagogue, during work, while visiting: always, the Jewish people repeated to God and each other their traditions and faith.

There were, as in any oral tradition, some people educated in literacy. They read the holy books and interpreted the lessons. But this was a very small number, proportionately, and in the Jewish society consisted only of rabbis and their students.

Jesus however, was neither an established rabbi nor

one of the selected students. The Jews were *genuinely* astonished when Jesus spoke publicly. 'How did he learn to read? He has not been taught.' They could not fathom the depth of his wisdom, nor locate its source by tracing the usual channels.

But Jesus was undeniably wise. His teaching was clear, direct and, most of all, extremely powerful. It created a furore, it stirred things up tremendously. It *changed* things. People got upset, or very enthusiastic. People refused to listen, or listened without ceasing. And if they listened, then they began changing. Nothing stayed the same when Jesus spoke.

Change is one of the most obvious results of a good teacher. It's impossible to limit the effect of powerful teaching, because it is both direct and indirect. The students themselves change, and then change the world. In this way the influence of powerful teaching is far-reaching. It stretches far beyond the individuals.

We see this is Jesus' life. *Taught by God*, he affected not only those he knew, but the world in which he lived. His impact continues today, shaping and reshaping our world.

How can we be taught by God, so we too can affect change?

Consider your motivation. Is it for your own or God's ends that you want to speak and accomplish? Sometimes people say, 'I don't know the difference between what I want and what God wants. Whatever I want must be bad.' Or, 'I can't really tell God's will. So I just do the best I can and hope it all works out.'

These insecurities aren't really necessary. We can learn from God in two very clear ways. The first is the scriptures, the second is the life of Jesus. The scriptures spell out God's intents and plans, Jesus embodies them. Our lives and desires can be checked against God's word, spoken through the Bible and through Jesus. We don't have to live in ignorance, but often it *is* easier.

Using God's word as a backdrop, think about yourself.

39

Is your character consistent with God's? Do you love, care, and serve, not seeking your own good first? Not hopefully, but *really*. Do you embody God's values: giving to those in need, sharing with the poor, inviting those who can't pay you back, refusing to gain at others' expense? Do your friendships, your budget, your possessions, your investments, your drinking habits, your ways of dealing with conflict, reflect God, or do they testify to the standards of society, do they witness to the ways of the world?

We can be taught by God, as Jesus was, but it means examining our motivations. It means admitting and giving up those which are not godly. It means changing our lives, not carrying on as if God hadn't spoken. It means allowing God to cleanse that which is selfish, which is nationalistic, which is narrow; it means allowing the Spirit to reveal that which is controlling, manipulative, fearful self-seeking. It means really relying on God and the truth of God's word, for we will be re-arranging our lives accordingly.

We can be taught by God. The Spirit will transform, instruct, educate. If we learn from God, the world will be astonished, as with Jesus. 'How can this be?' people will say. 'It is not by the usual means.'

They will be right. Our teaching will not be from ourselves, it will be from the God who sent Jesus. Like him, we will have learnt by other means.

Prayer

God and father of all,
Teach me your ways. Make me wise, discerning, diligent. Teach me by your Spirit. Help me to be receptive and a good learner. Help me to be a good listener. In Jesus' name. Amen.

Practice

Get two pamphlet copies of a gospel, and give one each to people whom you know are interested in learning about Christ.

Day 9

Jesus Knows God as Companion

'. . . *BECAUSE I am not alone: the one who sent me is with me . . .' 'They did not recognise that he was talking to them about the Father. So Jesus said: When you have lifted up the Son of man, then you will know that I am He and that I do nothing of my own accord. What I say is what the Father has taught me; he who sent me is with me, and has not left me to myself, for I always do what pleases him.'* (John 8:16, 27–29)

Think of a winding road through a forest. It is dark: evening has ceased, and the night noises and strange sounds are much clearer now that the beauty of the sunset is gone.

Before you were comfortable, walking silently, praising the mellow golden light, the surprising scarlet and lavender skies, the soft sounds of scurrying creatures. Now it is not so nice. In fact, it is actually unpleasant. The cool of the day has turned to chilling cold, the absence of light makes you feel unsure. The strange sounds now make you nervous, you walk more quickly and look up sharply, wondering what may come suddenly from the black wood either side.

What would you like most in this moment? What would relax and reassure you?

For many, it would be a companion. Another person, another presence, another voice, mind, personality. Someone to share the uncertainty and divide the apprehension. Things would be very different then: the animals wouldn't seem so alien, the noises not so portentous, the dark not so pervasive. Nor would the uncertainties of the black road, winding ahead, have quite so much power. It wouldn't matter that it was unfamiliar, its twists and turns so unpredictable in the darkness. Traversing it would take on the nature of an adventure. It could cease to be an inevitable obstacle.

Jesus' life, like our own, was a journey through light and dark. Sometimes he could see clearly, so progress was apparent; othertimes the way was very dark, not illuminated at all by familiar, helpful landmarks. Still he continued.

He did not continue alone, however. According to his own words, 'I am not alone: the one who sent me is with me.' Jesus had a companion on his pilgrimage: he had that other person, that other presence, that other voice, mind and personality, that helped, supported, relaxed, reassured.

In his relationship with God, Jesus experienced a friendship and fellowship that enabled him to continue his chosen path, despite the darkness, the strange sounds, the unwelcome twists and turns. Jesus knew God's constant companionship. He experienced God's constant welcome, God's constant encouragement, friendship and care. These enabled Jesus to live with himself and others in a way that was constant in its turn, continually witnessing to God's presence, God's involvement, God's love.

A companion is a special kind of friend. There is a depth and breadth to companionship which doesn't exist in every friendship.

Many friendships develop for particular reasons. While they are enjoyable within their own limits, they do not go beyond them. Some friendships are practical: we take each other's children on alternate days, we form car pools to save time and expense, we shop together because we value a second opinion. Other friendships are social. We enjoy the same activities or entertainments, but do not discuss finances or personal difficulties; we like the same foods but steer away from political conversations.

Friendships which include companionship, however, have an aspect of wholeness. There are no limits, personal or social. There are no barriers, no hurdles. Companions are silent or vocal, assertive or disinclined, active or passive, as suits the moment. Whatever the mode, the relationship remains the same. There is a steadiness unaffected by the changing rhythm of current events.

Companionship is like a deep well of clear, pure water. There is stillness because of the depth, there is depth because of the acceptance, there is acceptance because of the security.

One does not have to be or do: one is, and that is enough. And more than enough, it is perfect. One is valued by virtue of one's very being.

How does companionship grow between two people? How can we know God as Jesus did, in silent or spoken depth?

If we look at his life, we see that Jesus made it a priority to spend time with God.

He arranged his life so that he could be with God, so he could speak with God, so he could listen to God. Jesus often went to 'a quiet place', 'rose up early to pray', was 'found in a remote place.'

To be companions is to offer to the other the same time that is offered to one, to learn how to respect even as one is respected, to learn to wait and listen even as one is waited upon and listened to. It's to give the necessary time and attention to learn what the other person is like, what the other prefers, what the other desires. It's to know each other very well. It's to honour, accept, reverence what the other holds dear, finds important, cares for.

Companionship is a mutual relationship. Each gives, each receives, each takes, each asks. Each speaks, each listens, each responds, each questions, each answers.

44

Jesus' companionship with God was not one-sided. Jesus offered God a rich relationship, for Jesus loved knowing God, listening to God, conversing with God, hearing and accepting God's ideas, God's intents, God's hopes. It must have delighted God to have Jesus as a companion, to teach Jesus, to be with him, to 'not leave him to himself.'

There is some of the contemplative in companionship. Time becomes a different creature, leaping smoothly and invisibly, gone before its proper measure. Time becomes rich and full, a treasure doubly valued because it vanishes so quickly. The hours pass like minutes yet they are singular almost beyond description, able to be traced clearly and simply. One can recall, 'First we did this, then we did that, then we did that.' Mysteriously, the complex exchange of love, joy, security and satisfaction is easily refined, reduced to its seemingly simple parts.

Companionship is a great gift, a unique experience of friendship. Let us experience it as Jesus does, giving ourselves to God, making time for God, sitting or striding in mutual relationship with God. The light of Christ shines on our dark roads, lighting the way for companionship with God.

Prayer

Lord of light, Lord of Love,
How attractive you are, how much I long to be closer to you! Help me plan my time, so I have more to spend with you. I want our relationship to grow and deepen. I want to be as close to you as John was to Jesus, leaning on his breast, resting in his love, delighting in his very being. Amen.

Practice

Plan a half or whole day away from your regular routines. Go to a retreat centre, a park or the seaside, by yourself. Spend the time quietly with God, thinking, praying, walking, reading the scriptures, talking aloud if you like.

Day 10

Jesus Knows God as Redeemer

---

*A*S *Jesus went along, he saw a man who had been blind from birth. His disciples asked him, 'Rabbi, who sinned, this man or his parents, that he should have been born blind?' 'Neither he nor his parents sinned,' Jesus answered, 'he was born blind so that the works of God might be revealed in him.' . . . Having said this, he spat on the ground, made a paste with the spittle, put this over the eyes of the blind man, and said to him, 'Go and wash in the Pool of Siloam (the name means 'one who has been sent'). So he went off and washed and came back able to see. (John 9:1–3, 6–7)*

Did God deliberately afflict this man with blindness? Could it be?

We believe God loves, cares, sacrifices. Why would God intentionally, seemingly maliciously, afflict an innocent, indeed helpless creature? And apparently for God's own glory?

What about the man? What about his life, what about his feelings? Does God suppose it's a small thing to be unable to see? To be able to function fully as an adult? To be unable to seek usual employment, perhaps to have the choice of marriage and children taken away, prevented by disability? Does *none* of this matter?

Recently, we spent much time in prayer for a young man nearly fatally injured in a motor accident. It was a bizarre mishap, absolutely strange, and left a 27 year old married man its victim. There was no hope given that he would ever again think, feel, walk. His life, if such a word could still be used, was hopeless. It was finished.

And so we prayed, time after time, day after day. All this raised questions. If God loves, why does God allow these things? If God promises security, why doesn't God protect? Did God intend this? But God is supposed to intend good. Is it easier or harder to be a Christian when tragedy erupts? Can one really rage at God, releasing all the confusion and fear, or does this make one feel more confused, feel guilty?

Questions are inevitable when there is suffering, accident, tragedy. Jesus' disciples had questions as soon as they saw the blind man. 'How did this happen?' they asked. 'Who sinned? Who can be blamed?'

Jesus' answer was surprising. *No one* was sinful, *no one* could be blamed. This affliction, Jesus said, 'would reveal the works of God.'

This would be so because the works of God are most often revealed through people. And not people in isolation, but people in relationship to God.

God's works are rarely sovereign. They are accomplished because of a partnership between God and people. If people will be involved with God, seek God, listen to God, enquire of God, pursue God, God's ability to work is released. God is, as it were, empowered to be God.

If people perceive God as God, honour God as God, acknowledge God as God, worship God as God, God's desire to love, heal and redeem is released. For God is being perceived as a person, a very powerful person, a unique person. God is being understood, appreciated and encouraged in his gifts and personality. This relationship releases God to be himself most fully. It breaks down the barriers which imprison God in heaven, preventing him from redeeming evil on earth.

The question about the man born blind was not one of right or wrong, it was one of *access*. Could God have access to that man's life? If so, God could and would act like God, healing, loving, redeeming. If not, God was

47

prevented from working, prevented from doing what he longed to do.

There's nothing wrong with questioning God. It's good to question: we come closer to who God really is, we come into contact with our own power to release God to work in our lives and in the world.

But the real question is, will we let God be God? Will we turn to God whatever our circumstances, tragic or painful, glorious or ordinary? Will we give God access, so God's redemption can be experienced and seen? Will we allow *all* of life to reveal God's works?

God has questions too, but they're not like ours. God doesn't ask, 'Who sinned? Who is to blame?' Sin and failure are not problems for God'. He is able to forgive sin, restore injustice, shed mercy. God asks, 'Who will join me, who will accept me? Who will live by love, as I do? Who will accomplish my will? Who will work with me?'

Jesus healed the blind man, using his saliva and the dust around him, using the water from one of the local fountains. God, using the sweat and ground and water of our lives, using the hopes, prayers and questions of our hearts, will also heal. Our friend, an impossible case medically, a hopeless case scientifically, lay in an endless coma, until the doctors advised all the intensive care be stopped. It could not avail. More questions, more prayer. Then the next day, the man opened his eyes and saw. He recognised his wife and spoke softly but distinctly. Now he walks, talks, loves. He is living: the works of God revealed in him.

Prayer

Lord,

I want to give you access to my life. I want to know your love and redemption in every circumstance.

If my life shatters suddenly from tragedy, help me to stay near you. If events are hostile and not what I'd expected, help me to pursue you. If things happen that

I don't understand and hate, help me to hear you. Speak to me, teach me, comfort me, so my love and trust for you are always deepening. Amen.

Practice

Think of one way God has redeemed you, one event or situation which he has 'bought back'. Make a point of telling a friend your story.

PART TWO:

ABRAM HEARS GOD
BOOK OF GENESIS

Day 11

Abram Hears God in Daily Life

---

*T*HE Lord said to Abram, 'Leave your country, your
kindred and your father's house for a country which
I shall show you; and I shall make you a great nation. I
shall bless you and make your name famous; you are to
be a blessing!' . . . So Abram went as the Lord told him.
(Genesis 12:1–2, 42)

Saturdays are often good days for working in the garden,
shopping or cleaning out cupboards, for watching sports
or old films on television in the afternoon. Sundays are
sometimes good for washing the car, but more often, for
visiting with relatives or reading the papers, for a walk
in the park or drive in the country. Sunday evenings
tend to be rushed, especially if the children have left
their homework or you have to prepare for the work
week ahead.

Weekdays have their own routine. Catch a train, rush
for the bus, squash on the tube. Feed the children, find
the school ties, fish out the gym shorts. Collect the cook,
pay the local bills, drop the dog at the vet.

For others, time is not so pressing. It doesn't matter
when you get to the Job Centre because there's no work

going anyway. Or there are so many people for so few jobs that it's useless to queue at all. So down to the shops and hang around the lamp-post. Or have a lie-in, and then over to the pub after the betting shop.

What was Abram doing when God spoke to him for the first time? Was he just finishing breakfast, was he talking with the shepherds about the new lambs? Was he managing the family business with Lot, was he watching Sarai organise the household servants? Was it a weekend, a change from the daily routine, or just weekday life as usual?

There was no roar of thunder, Abram wasn't suddenly surrounded by a mysterious darkness, he wasn't transported to a dimension transcending time, space or usual definition. The scriptures just say that *God spoke*.

Reflect on the pattern of your life. Where would you be in one of your most usual moments? What would you be doing in one of your most ordinary activities?

Imagine God speaking to you suddenly, as to Abram. And not just a casual word, not just a friendly greeting or some helpful advice, but a shocking directive which shatters your routine and will change your whole life. What would be the most surprising time at which God might speak? And how would you respond?

If you were amazed, would it be because God spoke, or because God spoke when everything was so normal? Just another Thursday . . . cars passing on the street as usual, or cows clumping down the lane . . . nothing different from the way things always are. Cars, cows, telephones, trains, jobs, no jobs . . . ordinary, normal, daily life. Predictable life, expected life. But God's speaking in the midst of them: unpredictable, unexpected?

If so, why?

God created earth, time and space: why are we surprised that God uses them, that God speaks into them? True, God transcends time; but we don't. True, God is not limited to space; but for the most part, we are. Where can God find us, if not in our daily lives? Where, if not in the ordinariness and usualness, the normality, of our regular routines?

For that is where we live. That is where we are to be found. We have no other time than the present, that's why we fill it with responsibilities, friendships, activities. We have no other place than our usual contexts: home, office, school, streets, cars, buses. They are where we live.

God willingly enters into our daily lives. For this is the God of the Incarnation, the God of life who joins us on earth. God willingly relates to us as we wash the dishes, work in the office, travel back and forth, collect the children, go to a movie, work for charity, go to a disco, buy a lamp. For this is the God who gave Jesus to us, the God who sent the beloved Son to live with us. God willingly speaks in time and space, for this is the God who is creator: and all things, time, space, people, are the creatures of his hand.

All had been created by God and for God. But we make of our lives a human Eden, barring God out. We draw a circle of limited circumference, and place God outside. We are surprised, even shocked or stunned, that God speaks to us in our usual situations.

It's not unusual that God would speak, what's unusual is that we find God's speaking in daily life unexpected.

Prayer

Lord,

Enliven my expectation! I want you to speak to me, and I want to hear you clearly and well. Meet me in my daily life, help me recognise you in my work, be close to me as I solve the many large and small problems which turn up each day. Amen.

Practice

Today or tomorrow, be alert for God to speak to you, showing a way you can help someone then and there, at school, work or home. Do what is needed.

Day 12

Abram Hears God in Anticipation

'. . . *AND I shall make you a great nation, I shall bless you and make your name famous; you are to be a blessing!*' (Genesis 12:2)

Because God's call to Abram seems so extreme, we might easily concentrate on its hardship, its challenge. Then we'd get discouraged, because we'd have made Abram a hero of such stature that we become pygmies. *Our* obedience to God would seem laughable. Soon we'd conclude that we needn't obey God at all.

Yes, Abram was remarkable. He was also no fool.

Consider what God offered him. It was a phenomenal package, an excellent proposition. One which, whatever the risks, any intelligent, or adventurous, or ambitious, or just plain *sensible* person would be foolish to turn down.

I shall make you a great nation. The word 'nation' has a definite meaning, whatever one's culture. It immediately implies authority and power. It indicates geography and place, ownership of land. It includes a people, a whole population, not just one family.

Further, this was to be a 'great' nation. This is very plain. Great nations are wealthy, dominant over their enemies, successful. They are secure, famous, glorious, envied, feared, respected.

Next, God spoke of blessing Abram. Who wouldn't want to be blessed? Blessed by anyone, but especially a god. In particular, by *this* God, reputed to be more powerful than any other. For blessing imparts fulfilment, satisfaction, peace, security, wholeness, protection, wealth, riches. Blessing means length of life, richness of life, fecundity of life, abundance of life.

And fame! God offered Abram more than just personal gain, he offered historical prominence. Abram would become a star. His name captured in history, his adventures described far and wide, his actions extolled, admired, envied.

God's last promise was that Abram himself would be a blessing. This is more mysterious, but certainly attractive. How wonderful, to give wealth, fruitfulness, satisfaction to others. Just how this could happen Abram didn't know, for blessing was usually given through the family line. The father laid hands on his sons, 'blessing', bringing to life with words the potential in each person, passing on the wealth of his own life. Abram, however, had no children. But why refuse something just because it's not understood?

Think again about what Abram was taking with him. He was not leaving behind his wife, his possessions or even all his relatives. His marriage was important to God: it was together with Sarai that Abram went forth. Nor did God say, as he sometimes does, Leave all your possessions. Abram took goods, servants, slaves, flocks and herds. Even Lot his nephew, and all his belongings, went along.

Abram did have to think gravely about what he was leaving. But look what was offered! If he would take the chance, take a risk . . . look what waited!

How important it is to hear both sides of what God says. Not to separate the painful, the hard, the unpleasant from the promise, the offer, the fulfilment. When God asks us to open our hands, releasing what is dear, it is so we can receive what is even more precious. If we clench our fists, holding, protecting, we cannot grasp what God would give. Our potential is cut off, our possibilities prevented. If we cannot relinquish, we cannot receive.

God in Christ offers us the riches of creation, the wealth of heaven, fullness of life.

God gives love, pours out mercy, casts aside fear. God gives authority to bind and loose, establish truth, displace deception. God promises peace that passes understanding, security that cannot be shattered, confidence that will not fail.

God offers friendship and family life, dwelling with us and in us; God gives the Spirit, to renew, empower and release us. God gives houses, brothers, sisters, mothers, children, land, eternal life – as well as persecution. God blesses those who give all for Christ, and their lives bless others, God's riches spilling over.

God offers everything, all he has. In giving everything to follow Christ, remember what God promises you.

Hear God, perceive what will be given: obey, so that you can receive.

Prayer

Dear God,

Show me more of your plan for my life. Help me hear the whole of your word. Release my spirit to respond fully to you. Widen my understanding, so I will bring blessing to others. In Jesus' Name, Amen.

Practice

To express appreciation for what God has given you, what God has done for you, plan a small celebration for family or friends. Bake a cake, pick some flowers, light a candle, play a song.

Day 13

Abram Hears God in Obedience

SO Abram went as the Lord told him, and Lot went with him. Abram was seventy-five years old when he left Haran. Abram took his wife Sarai, his nephew Lot, all the possessions they had amassed and the people they had acquired in Haran. They set off for the land of Canaan, and arrived there. (Genesis 12:4–5)

On the face of it, God's word to Abram was stark. *Leave your country, your kindred and your father's house for a country which I shall show you.*

If God said something that strange, that strong, that uprooting to you, what would happen?

Pause, and put yourself in your current situation, into that position. Hear God speak those same words to you. Hear God speak your name, then continue:

Leave this country. Leave this home, this national identity, this land where you know the language, the politics, the money, the customs.

Leave your kindred. Leave your relatives, your friends, those of 'like kind'. Leave those familiar relationships of birth and blood, leave those warm friendships of the heart, which support you, encourage you, ground you.

Leave your father's house. Leave your natural environment. Leave your home, with its lonely or cheery rooms, leave your crowded noisy streets or your quiet lanes, leave the river or sea or streams where you walk, swim, fish.

Leave. Leave it all. Now.

What do you feel?

What do you think?

How could this work?

How do you decide whether to obey God's word? Do you have a choice at all or does the mere fact of having heard God mean an automatic assent? Who do you talk with? Who do you tell? How do you prepare for an unknown destination? What arrangements must you make first?

For us, the above may only be theoretical. But for Abram it was much more than an exercise of imagination. It was entirely real. Everything he was leaving was familiar, traditional and secure. What he was going to was unknown.

Even God was unknown. This God who spoke to Abram was a God from the distant past, known by ancient relatives like Noah. This God's activity and power were part of history. They were in the mythology, they were part of a broad religious heritage which had only the slightest impact on Abram's current life. In leaving all that was familiar, predictable and secure, Abram was doing so in relation to a God who was unfamiliar, alive only in remote tradition, apparently offering only risk and insecurity.

But Abram chose to obey. And of his own free will, from his own desire.

We could pretend that Abram didn't really have a choice. We could argue that God was so powerful Abram was overwhelmed. For if the Lord of all creation, the God of space and sky and depths and heights, speaks, we can say it is such a momentous event, there is such power, such charisma, in the personality, that it would be impossible to gainsay this Person. But truly, we know that people can and do – indeed, we ourselves can and do – hear and ignore God all the time. History is a bitter trail littered with the disasters of human ignorance and rejection of God.

Abram, because he heard and *obeyed* God, is remarkable. God was explicit with him, naming one by one all the powerful, earthly things that give identity and security: and Abram released those possessions to obey God. Abram had all the things in which we trust, yet he chose to trust God instead. Abram had to think, feel, evaluate and plan, to obey God; yet no feeling, no rationalising, no impediment, was stronger than his decision to do so.

This obedience has caused Abram to be called 'the father of our faith.' Parents are meant to accept responsibility, to raise the young to maturity, to lead and guide. Abram, in his obedience to God, is indeed a parent to us. We can follow his direction, we can look clearly at life and make the same choices of faith he made, we can choose God as our first security. Abram is an example and a model.

Abram heard and obeyed God; we are his children if we do the same. Abram risked all, to receive the inheritance God promised; from him, we inherit the faith which trusts God first, last and all the time in between.

Leave, Abram. And he did. So should we.

Prayer

Lord,
I want to obey you. But I must hear you, to know how. Speak by your Spirit, quicken the scriptures to me, let me recognise your voice in the voices of others.

Help me hear and obey, help me trust and release. Amen.

Practice

Make a list of all the scriptures which have encouraged you on your journey of faith.

Day 14

Abram Hears God in Trust

THE Lord said to Abram after Lot had parted company from him, 'Look all around from where you are, to north and south, to east and west, for all the land within sight I shall give to you and your descendants for ever. I shall make your descendants like the dust on the ground: when people succeed in counting the specks of dust on the ground, then they will be able to count your descendants too. On your feet! Travel the length and breadth of the country, for I mean to give it to you.' (Genesis 13:14–17)

Following Abram this far, we see that he, Lot and all their households left the family land, travelled to Canaan, continued on to Bethel and eventually settled on the Negeb River. Driven by famine, they moved temporarily to Egypt, then retraced their way: back to the Negeb, back to Bethel.

At that point, Abram realised that the land couldn't sustain both households. He generously offered Lot first choice for re-location. 'Is not the whole land open before you?' he said to his nephew. 'Go in the opposite direction to me: if you take the left, I will go right; if you take the right, I will go left.' Lot chose the best land which was 'irrigated and looked like the garden of God.'

It was then that God spoke again. Re-read what was said.

What is noticeable is that God told Abram nothing new. No further revelation, no additional communication, no new information. God only repeated what had been said before, elaborating with certain specifics.

Granted, it was good that God spoke at all. But at this

time in Abram's life, the *content* of God's speaking would be very important. Surely Abram longed for fresh encouragement, for words to give him new heart.

Recall the changes, the transitions, the hardships Abram and company had endured. Moving scores of people, family, servants and slaves; shifting hundreds of herds, thousands of sheep, cattle and other livestock; sorting out, packing up, putting down, settling in. Time and again, from Haran to Canaan to Bethel to the Negeb to Egypt to the Negeb to Bethel. Sorting out family problems, accommodation, arguments between the herdsmen; working out the routes, so the caravans would always be near water when it was necessary, near settlements when supplies needed replenishing.

Then, because their combined wealth was now so great, it was practical for Abram and Lot to part. The result was that Lot took the best land, leaving Uncle Abram with the not-so-good.

After *years* of change, transition and hardship, wouldn't it be a relief to settle down? Wouldn't it be wonderful to hear God say, 'Here it is, this is it! You've arrived! This is the place I promised, it's to this that I've called you. Stop! Stop now, stay here.'

But God didn't say that. God only repeated the original intention. Worse, God finished with, 'On your feet! Travel the length and breadth of the country, for I mean to give it to you.' And we read 'So Abram moved his tent . . .'

Sometimes, our pilgrimage of obedience is as confusing as it is clear. Sometimes, when we want to settle, God tells us to keep moving. Sometimes, when we only want to unpack and relax, God says to keep things together and keep going.

Sometimes, when we have been in change, transition and hardship intolerably long, God's word will not relieve us. It will not give the settled relief for which we long.

Rather, we hear with Abram, 'On your feet! Travel

the length and breadth of the country.' Whatever our 'country', whatever 'travel' means for us – whether it be friendships that have come apart, a family member who is dying, a job that is unpleasant but necessary, an actual relocation that still will not be permanent – whatever our own situation is, we find ourselves in the same position as Abram. We have the same choice. Will we obey?

The encouraging part is that God often speaks again, repeating what was said, perhaps adding a few details. The hard part is that your basic situation will not yet be changed. You will have to remain, when you would rather be released.

You have to continue to trust God with all your heart, all your strength, all your mind, will and feelings. Like Abram, you have to continue with the word already heard. You have to trust God *will* lead you through your unknown country, you have to trust God *does* 'mean to give it to you.'

Prayer

God of pilgrims, travel with me.
Lord of change, keep me stable.
Spirit of hope, take my despair.
God, Lord, Spirit, help me hear, trust, persevere. Amen.

Practice

Read Proverbs 3:5–6. Re-phrase it in your own words.

Day 15

Abram Hears God in Fear

*S*OME *time later, the word of the Lord came to Abram
in a vision:
'Do not be afraid Abram!
I am your shield
and shall give you a very great reward.' (Genesis 15:1)*

God is often a person of few words. But just one word
or phrase may address a multitude of fears. It can settle
a host of doubts, apprehensions, confusions, insecurities.
So with these few words to Abram.

Abram heard God in a vision, which means that either
physically or mentally God appeared. Abram saw God.
Abram heard God. God *initiated* a relationship with him.
God reached out, Abram was not left alone.

Next, God spoke directly to Abram's need. God *defined*
Abram's situation. Fear is crippling, enervating and
debilitating; fear is one of the most powerful and potentially controlling emotions we can experience. God recognised Abram's emotional state and named it aloud. In
naming Abram's affliction, God exposed it. In defining
it, God by the Spirit exercised authority over it.

God spoke to Abram personally, by *name*. God didn't
call him 'my obedient servant', 'my faithful follower',
my courageous supporter', although all that was true.
God called him by name, 'Abram'.

We always call our friends by name. We express affec-
tion, delight, warmth, concern, care, by speaking
personally to those we love. So does God, the creator of
all persons, the author of every personality.

Then God *reassured* Abram. Having defined his situation, God supplied what was necessary to change it. 'I am your shield' God said. This was a literal statement. Again, what God *didn't* say is significant. God *didn't* say, 'I am like a shield' or 'I am as a shield'. God put himself directly into Abram's life, declaring protection: 'I *am* your shield.'

We don't know what Abram feared. Was it the hostile tribes surrounding him? Was it threat of another famine? Was it hopeless depression because he had been faithful and obeyed God, yet still he had no child to succeed him and fulfil God's plans? Was he increasingly desperate, struggling with the apparent reality that God's word was not going to be accomplished? Whatever Abram's fear, God promised himself as protection.

Finally, God promised Abram 'a great *reward*'. God is generous, God wants to give a full measure in return for faith and obedience. God wants Abram to have a just recompense for all his hardship, sorrow and sacrifice.

God is not malicious. God doesn't take our lives, our hopes, our trust, then regard them lightly. God does not use us casually for private purposes. God does not violate our personality, our potential for many directions in life. God respects and honours, God does not take for granted, those who accept his values, choose his way, living according to his word.

God wants to assure Abram that his hope is not in vain. God is a just person, and justice will be accomplished. God is not only generous but powerful: Abram will be rewarded.

Sometimes we hear God frequently, othertimes it seems we never hear God at all. Remember, God can be a person of few words. Yet those spare sentences will contain an unfathomable depth of love and care. Listen for God's words, which *initiate*, *define*, *name*, *reassure*, *reward*.

Prayer

Jesus said, Your almsgiving must be secret, and your Father who sees all that is done in secret will reward you.

Lord, Let my giving be secret, and not self-seeking.

Jesus said, When you pray, go to your private room, shut yourself in, and so pray to your Father who is in that secret place, and your Father who sees all that is done in secret will reward you.

Lord, Let my prayers seek you truly, and let their fruit be service to the world you love.

Jesus says, When you fast, put scent on your head and wash your face, so that no one will know you are fasting except your Father who sees all that is done in secret; and your Father who sees all that is done in secret will reward you.

Lord, teach me to fast: from food and drink, from distraction, from avoiding painful truths.

Jesus says, Anyone who has ears for listening should listen!

Lord, let me hear and obey you. Free me from my fear. Let me trust in your justice. Amen.

Practice

Look carefully, today or tomorrow, at the people you see daily. Notice if someone is habitually anxious or nervous. Pray for them each day for a week.

Day 16

Abram Hears God in Uncertainty

'*LORD God,' Abram replied, 'what use are your gifts, as I am going on my way childless? . . . Since you have given me no offspring,' Abram continued, 'a member of my household will be my heir.' (Genesis 15:2)*

How direct Abram is! He answers God plainly and straight from his heart.

'What use are your gifts?' How many people have the strength of personality to say that to God? Usually we're *seeking* God's gifts, seeking grace, revelation, reassurance, prophecy, direction, understanding, confirmation, knowledge, wisdom, blessing, power, benefits.

But Abram wasn't. He merely wanted to know how life was going to work practically. God had promised to bless him and his descendants, and there were no descendants. What use gifts? What use reward or recompenses? Abram wanted a child, an heir of flesh and blood.

Abram is as direct with God as God is with him. There is no false apprehension: Abram speaks straightforwardly. There is no fawning: Abram doesn't flatter or pacify God. There is no insecurity or mumbling 'humility': Abram hears what God says and then answers.

Abram's response reveals several truths about his relationship with God.

He calls God 'Lord Almighty', proving that he knew to whom he spoke. This wasn't some obscure tribal god or powerful local deity that might prevent Abram's success in his adopted land. This was GOD: the creator of all things, the omnipotent and mysterious Lord, the one whose name was so sacred as to be unpronounceable. Abram was involved with GOD: and he knew it.

Abram next acknowledges God's promise of great reward. He doesn't reject it, but he's not overly impressed. He questions its usefulness, for it doesn't seem to touch the real issue.

Which is exactly that, the question of issue. Abram has been married for years, and he and Sarai have no children. They had none before they heard and obeyed God, they have had none since. Yet children, or at least one child, are essential for God's word to be worked out on earth.

Lastly, Abram put the responsibility for his childlessness entirely onto God. 'Since you have given me no offspring', he says. The question of life is in God's hands: and what is God doing about it? Abram and Sarai are powerless to procreate, and they know it. If there will be any fruitfulness of the flesh from their union, the seed must be planted by God. And it hasn't been.

The only alternative is for Abram to have an heir by customary Mesopotamian tribal means. If a wedded wife could not bear children she could legitimately give a slave woman to her husband, to produce a child to continue the family line. Am I to be reduced to this? Abram asked God. Is that how your word will be fulfilled?

Abram was uncertain. He could not put together the puzzling pieces of his obedience to God. He could not see that God was creating the picture he had viewed by faith.

Abram was uncertain, but he communicated. He held back nothing from God. He opened his heart, he shared all his uncertainty and confusion. He was not ashamed, he did not disparage himself or his faith because he didn't know what God was doing. He didn't understand what was happening, but he didn't get angry and accuse God, he didn't malign and abuse God.

Neither did Abram spiritualise his uncertainty. He didn't convince himself it wasn't as bad as it seemed, he knew it was. He didn't comfort himself with the ready sop that God was God, after all – and who was he to question? He didn't keep a stiff upper lip and carry on; that was impossible, because his resources of hope and understanding had run low.

Abram did none of these things. He treated God like the powerful person he is, and carried on a conversation. Having listened to God's words, he now questioned their appropriateness. Having got straight what God was doing, he asked how it would meet his needs.

And the result of this honest, direct speaking in a time of uncertainty? Did God strike Abram down, roaring 'Who are you to question me, you desert mouse!'? Did God ignore Abram, remote in stony divine silence? Did God condemn Abram, pointing out that *his* was not to reason why?

What happens, if you speak your heart to God in a time of fearful uncertainty? What happens, if you don't hide your confusion?

To Abram, 'the Lord's word came in reply.' The same is true for us. Speaking our heart to God releases God's heart. Admitting our uncertainty frees God to reply.

Prayer

Jesus,
   Lead me closer to the God you know. I want to be like you and Abram, telling God all that I think, feel, fear and hope.
Spirit of God,
   Help me not to hide. Surround me through your presence, reveal God's love, so I am free with God. Quicken my ability to hear God's replies. Amen.

Practice

Recall one concern that troubles you greatly. Go to a field and pick up a rock, or to a wood and find a stick, or to a river or lake and fetch a stone. Talk to God, confessing your anxiety and asking to be released from it.

Then, imagining that your rock or stick or stone is your fear, throw it away from you as hard as you can.

Day 17

Abram Hears God in Faith

THEN the Lord's word came to him in reply, 'Such a one will not be your heir; no, your heir will be the issue of your own body.' Then taking him outside, he said, 'Look up at the sky and count the stars if you can. Just so will your descendants be,' he told him. Abram put his faith in the Lord and this was reckoned to him as uprightness. (Genesis 15:4–6)

Abram is the father of our faith because he heard God and chose to believe. He heard God and obeyed. In doing so, he was staking his whole life on God, uprooting all other security, severing every tie that would have bound him to the ways of the world.

Then he journeyed. He pilgrimaged. He sojourned, moving from place to place on his trek of obedience.

All this was done in faith. Abram listened and chose to believe: *he put his faith in the Lord.*

Putting one's faith in the Lord is an act of will. It is done by making a conscious decision. We hear God, understand what God is saying: and then determine whether or not we will respond.

Obedience to God is rarely an accident, a coincidence of time and space; obedience comes from a clear-cut decision.

Obedience to God cannot be a matter of happenstance. If so our obedience will always be at risk, for other events will change, pressurise, attack our decision.

Obedience to God cannot be based on how one feels. Our feelings are transient, they are as instable as water. They soar and plummet as circumstances change.

Abram is singular in honour and history because he chose to believe and obey God with practically no support. His only real resource was his own faith. There weren't others around who knew, heard, believed or obeyed God. Abram risked and ventured, alone in all the world. At the best of times it's not easy to believe God, everything militates against it. But Abram did, and at the worst of times.

We can too. In fact, we are far more fortunate than Abram. We have a wealth of ways to confirm God's word. We are not abandoned in a desert of faith, wandering in search of living water, living Word. We are blessed in time and space. With the fullness of history behind us, we benefit from generations of faith; we have countless examples to help, encourage and direct.

We have the scriptures, which make concrete God's word and actions in history. They tell the stories and experiences of faithful people, from Noah, David, Eve and Deborah, to Peter, Mary Magdalen and Lazarus, to Barnabas, Lydia, Onesimus . . . an endless list of people who heard, believed and obeyed God.

We have the life and death and risen life of Jesus. Jesus, the son of God, who was human as we are, flesh and blood as we are, whose faith changed the world and changes us. His words are set down, printed out – teaching, explaining, requiring. We have the gift of the Holy Spirit, the very life and nature of God, who dwells in the centre of our lives.

We have the grace of the sacraments and the tradition of the church. We have the lives of the saints; and the prayers and fellowship of the communion of saints. We have elders, faithful men and women of maturity whom we respect and to whom we give God's authority; we have brothers and sisters in Christ, members with us of the body of Christ. We share friendship, fellowship, a common hope, a common calling, a common life.

What riches these are, what support! What an encouragement! How fortunate we are, at this point in time and space, at this time in history. For we are called, just as Abram, to hear and believe, to hear and obey. If we avail ourselves well of this wealth from God, we need not doubt what God says. We can compare God's words and directions to God's word in scripture, Jesus and the saints. We can check our doubts against God's previous commands. We can be confirmed in our understanding and action by talking with wise and responsible Christians. Because their lives are submitted to God's word, we can trust their ability to direct and correct us as we make our personal pilgrimage of faith.

It is never easy to live with God, becoming aligned with God's ways and forsaking the world's. Abram did it however; and so can we. And we have graces Abram never dreamed of, to help us in *putting our faith in the Lord*.

Indeed, it was Abram's faithful response which released God's grace for us. He is the father of our faith. We are the descendants of Abram, numerous as the stars, just as God promised. Abram's faithful response released God's blessing for his own life; and his life has become a blessing for us, just as God promised.

Prayer

Lord,

To obey you I must hear you, to follow you I must be led by your Spirit. Speak clearly, let your voice become familiar to me. Empower me with the Spirit, so my faith will bear much fruit. Release me to discover the treasures of faith which you've given to encourage, guide and mature me. Amen.

Practice

Learn about a saint. Borrow or buy a book or tape, or talk with someone who can tell you the full story of the life of the person you've chosen.

73

Day 18

Abram Hears God in Confirmation

*H*E *then said to him, 'I am the Lord who brought you
out of Ur of the Chaldaeans to give you this country
as your possession.' (Genesis 15:7)*

'Who, why, what, where, when, how?'

These are the 'five W's and one H' that reporters
learn. They are a shorthand that summarise the facts
found in the opening paragraphs of newspaper articles.
In God's conversation with Abram there's also a shorthand. It's 'three P's, one T, one R.' Person, power,
purpose, time, relationship.

After Abram made his decision of will, – after he 'put
his faith in the Lord', – God *immediately* confirmed every
aspect of their relationship.

I am the Lord . . . God declared his identity, re-
affirming who he was.

God repeated his name. He wanted Abram to have no
doubt about the person with whom he was involved.
This was GOD: personal, real, the Lord of all.

. . . *who brought you out of Ur of the Chaldaeans* . . .
God declared his power, re-affirming what he'd done.

It was not by his own strength that Abram had travelled unharmed through foreign lands. It was not by his
own cleverness that Abram escaped death when living
temporarily in Egypt. It was not by his own might that
Abram had succeeded in alien countries, receiving gifts
of livestock and baskets of grain, occupying whatever
land he chose, living unmolested among pagans. It was
the LORD ALMIGHTY who had accomplished these
things. Abram had moved from one land to another,

from the place of his forebears to the place of his future: but it was God's power that had brought him out. God's power had secured his progress.

. . . *to give you this country as your possession.* God repeated his purpose, re-affirming his intent.

Abram had been drawn by God's promise, now God repeated that it was unchanged. Abram was to be blessed and to be a blessing, to share in the riches of heaven, to experience the miracles of God in his own flesh. Abram was to receive a land from God, he was to possess what had not been his. This possession would guarantee everything: stability, sustenance, security. Land assured a secure future, a family home, an inheritance to give to the next generation. God had promised all this, now God confirmed his commitment to accomplish it.

I am the Lord who brought you out of Ur of the Chaldaeans to give you this country as your possession.

This single sentence included and reviewed the whole of Abram's life. God acknowledged Abram's past, God accompanied Abram in the present, God affirmed Abram's future. This man had come from Ur, and although now in transit, would certainly be settled. God would do it.

What a relief for Abram when God reassured him so clearly! For we live in time, our lives are defined by its passing. Perhaps we are unhappy with our present, waiting for a bleak spell to end. Perhaps we look back, feeling the pleasures of the past, forgetting the unpleasant parts. Or maybe our current life is satisfactory but there's apprehension about the future. Of course things *won't* stay the same, but just how much will they change?

Because time is such a powerful creature, our faith must assure us that God actually holds it. God must tame it, God must contain it. We don't want God outside time, we must experience God in its passage.

These few but comprehensive words to Abram recognise this need. God repeated not only Abram's history but their *shared* history. 'I' and 'you' are said time and again. *I* am Yahweh: I am speaking to *you*, Abram. *I* brought *you*, *I* will give *you* this country.

God repeated to Abram the reality of their relationship in time. Abram had never been alone, God had always been with him. God had never wanted to be alone, he had invited Abram to join him. Indeed, God could not accomplish his aims alone: he chose Abram to work with him.

God's purposes for earth are not solitary. They are impossible to achieve without personal involvement. God's desire, from the beginning, is to know and be known, to love and be loved, to give and receive, share and be shared with, care and be cared for.

Three P's, then, and one T, one R. Person, power, purpose, time, relationship. God confirms it all, if we choose him as he has chosen us.

Prayer

Lord,
Please keep working with my will.

Please reveal more of your ways to me, so I can choose them and forsake my own. Please keep showing me your purposes, so I can put my power into them. Please deepen my understanding of your intents, so I can give more time to accomplishing them.

Please confirm that you are always with me, Lord of my past, present and future. Amen.

Practice

Using the 'five W's and one H' as a guide, tell a child the story of how you became involved with God.

Day 19

Abram Hears God in the Unexpected

'LORD God,' Abram replied, *'how can I know that I shall possess it?'* He said to him, *'Bring me a three-year-old heifer, a three-year-old she-goat, a three-year-old ram, a turtledove and a young pigeon.'* (Genesis 15:8–9)

It must have surprised Abram that God told him to prepare for worship. They were right in the middle of a conversation, there had been questions and answers going back and forth; suddenly, Abram is to find and prepare gifts for offering. Surely not the answer Abram was expecting, when he asked 'How can I *know* that I will possess this country?'

This sort of thing sometimes happens with people. We ask something, and they respond in a quite unexpected manner. If it's someone we know well, like a husband or wife, an intimate friend or relative, a close co-worker, we usually feel we can predict their answer. How shocking when it's completely different!

So with God. God is utterly unique and cannot be second-guessed. God is reliable and dependable: but God's answers should not be predicted. Nor should we limit the sort of response we expect. God may send us off in an entirely new direction, as he did Abram.

God is a God of darkness as well as light, of mystery as well as declaration, of transcendence as well as incarnation. God will speak through silence, God will respond by refusal, God will catch us up in heavenly heights as well as descend to earthly depths. God is both with us and beyond us, God is before and after us. God orders

77

time but is not confined to it, God commands angels to works of power that our minds cannot comprehend.

God didn't change the subject with Abram. God re-focused the sight-lines, redirecting Abram's attention. Why?

God knew the reassurance Abram sought would be effective only if Abram was in the right setting. Sitting in a tent, standing under the starry skies – these were inappropriate. So God shifted the scene. He told Abram to prepare for worship, to enter an environment which would help him receive the reassurance he needed.

What *consideration* on God's part. What sensitivity to Abram's creatureliness. As humans we are greatly susceptible to our surroundings. We react to atmosphere, environment, context. Our perception is easily inter-rupted by distractions, our comprehension clouded by movements, sounds, colours.

We are creatures of change and stimulation, but also of habit and stability. We enjoy surprise and challenge, we also need security and ritual. Our lives must be grounded in the familiar or we cannot cope with the foreign; certain places or actions must be primarily unch-anging, so we can stand the shocks of growth. In telling Abram to worship, God was creating an environment in which Abram would hear him without distraction.

Worship is a concentrated experience. In worship we consciously determine to focus on God. In worship we wait before God, choosing to let all other demands, press-ures, people, wait.

When we enter a home, it's because we want to spend time with the people there. So with worship. When we enter into it, it is to spend time with God. It is to give ourselves to God, to receive from God. That is why we are there.

In life we hear, believe and obey God; in worship we do more. We honour God. We reverence God, we offer God particular gifts, we bow before God in homage that we give to no other person.

Worship is as important as any good work we do in God's name. In worship we come close to the heart of God, forsaking the endless beat of our daily demands. In worship we appreciate God, letting go for a while of our own need for appreciation. In worship we delight in God, savouring the Spirit's delicacy and strength, breathing in the Spirit's power and gentleness.

God respected Abram's need for reassurance. God wanted Abram to receive it, so he was directed to prepare for worship. Therein, he would find what he sought.

Prayer

Holy Spirit,
    Quicken God's presence to me. Create in my soul a dwelling place for God, create in my heart a longing to dwell in God. Lead me into worship, so I can receive from God. Amen.

Practice

Have everyone in your family or a small group of friends find something that symbolises their life. Perhaps a leaf, because one's a gardener, a piece of paper because one's a typist, a bit of chalk because one's a teacher, a hair slide because one's a girl, etc. Have each person show the others what they've brought, and say why they've chosen it. Then put them all in a big bowl in the centre, and offer them to God.

Day 20

Abram Hears God in Worship

'*LORD God,*' Abram replied, '*how can I know that I shall possess it?*' **He said to him, 'Bring me a three-year-old heifer, a three-year-old she-goat, a three-year-old ram, a turtledove and a young pigeon.'** (*Genesis 15:8–9*)

God was very specific about what Abram was to offer. God required an heifer, a she-goat and a ram, all of a certain age, and two types of birds.

God wasn't woolly about what he wanted. He chose things familiar to Abram, things which Abram could give without great effort. The offerings required by God were part of Abram's life.

God is just as specific with us. It might make us uncomfortable, but it is true. We don't have to *wonder* what would please God. God says clearly, in the scriptures, through the life of Jesus and by the Spirit in our hearts, what he desires.

Micah, speaking[11] to God's people thousands of years ago, summarised God's requirements: 'You have already been told what is right and what the Lord wants of you. Only this, to act justly, to love tenderly and to walk humbly with your God.' (Micah 6:8)

Moses, one of God's first prophets, was absolutely certain what God wanted: 'You must love the Lord your God with all your heart, with all your soul, with all your strength . . . The Lord your God is the one you must fear, him alone you must serve, his is the name by which you must swear.' (Deut. 6:5, 13)

Jesus, the enfleshment of God's word, was equally

sure of God's desires: 'But I say this to you who are listening: Love your enemies, do good to those who hate you, bless those who curse you, pray for those who treat you badly. To anyone who slaps you on one cheek, present the other cheek as well; to anyone who takes your cloak from you, do not refuse your tunic. Give to everyone who asks you, and do not ask for your property back from someone who takes it. Treat others as you would like people to treat you.' (Luke 6:27–31)

It's *to you who are listening* that Jesus speaks. It's plain what God desires and requires. But *do* we listen?

If God is the only person we fear, what position do we take regarding nuclear defense? If God will provide for us, why do we reclaim our stolen property? If we walk humbly with God, why must we assert our opinions and wills? If we would like to be treated well, why do we support governments which treat entire populations badly? Using money and violence, they oppress and deprive whole peoples. The lives of the poor subsidise a tiny corps of the wealthy.

And more locally. Do you accomplish good works but refuse those Gospel phrases which would uncover your hardness of heart? Are you busy and active in your church, but find yourself unable to sit quietly? You cannot wait, in silence and patience, for God. Do you give God your money rather than your time, or your time rather than your money? Do you continue in broken relationship with that dreadful aunt, in ironic judgement of that unbearable old spinster who controls the Spring Fete, in scorn and disdain for the gypsies who have turned up again?

It's *to you who are listening* that God speaks. God speaks plainly, as to Abram. God is *very* specific about what we offer and how we worship, and that these are possible from our daily lives. But do we listen? Can we afford to?

Prayer

Lord Jesus,
Saviour of all, save me from possessiveness.

Redeem me, from the ways of the world, from the deceptions of my culture, from the pride which refuses to see others as sister and brother.

Fill me with your Spirit, so I am aware of being a member of the family of God. Lead me, into caring for others, living differently, so I am offering to you that which you've asked. For your sake, Lord, Amen.

Practice

Consider again the questions above. Select one area, and make a change in your life *now*.

PART THREE:

MARY LOVES GOD
LUKE'S GOSPEL

Day 21

Mary Loves God Simply

---

*I*N the sixth month the angel Gabriel was sent by God
. . . to a virgin betrothed to a man named Joseph, of
the House of David; and the virgin's name was Mary . . .
the angel said to her, 'Mary, do not be afraid; you have
won God's favour. Look! You are to conceive in your womb
and bear a son, and you must name him Jesus. He will
be great and will be called Son of the Most High. The
Lord God will give him the throne of his ancestor David;
he will rule over the House of Jacob for ever and his reign
will have no end.' Mary said to the angel, 'But how can
this come about, since I have no knowledge of man?' The
angel answered, 'The Holy Spirit will come upon you,
and the power of the Most High will cover you with its
shadow. And so the child will be holy and will be called
Son of God.' . . . Mary said, 'You see before you the
Lord's servant, let it happen to me as you have said.'
(Luke 1:6, 31–36, 38)

Mary's meeting with Gabriel was potentially one of the
most complex experiences a human being could have. It
was dense, packed full. Every single sentence carried
great weight, imparted incredible information. The event

could have overwhelmed an experienced mystic, befuddled the average Jew. Yet Mary was never confused, never agitated.

Consider the elements compounding this experience.

First, the arrival of an *angel*. Prior to the birth of Christ, angelic appearances were rare. God frequently spoke to the Jews through dreams, visions and prophets, but angels were generally sent only to the most dire situations. Heavenly messengers usually saved people from imminent death, either from enemies or starvation.

Secondly, Mary was a *woman*. The Old Testament records only a few instances of women being crucial to God's plans. God worked mostly through men.

Thirdly, Mary was told God had *chosen* her. She had 'won God's favour.' Why? What had she done, what was she to do? Why had God singled her out?

Then Gabriel unleashed a flood of astonishing information. Mary would become pregnant, the child already had a gender, a name and a predestined future. Further, Gabriel used a stream of provocative names and titles which every Jew would have recognised and honoured instantly: *The throne of his ancestor David, the House of Jacob, Son of* the *Most High, Lord God*. There were also phenomenal statements about the child, power and time: *he will rule for ever, his reign will have no end*.

There were equally staggering statements about herself. Hear with Mary all the 'you's. *You* have won God's favour, *You* are to conceive in *your* womb, *you* must name him Jesus. The Holy Spirit will come upon *you*, the power of the Most High will cover *you* with its shadow. Not only would God's power do all this, but that power required Mary's participation. God wanted to use Mary's very body, soul and spirit.

Within the space of a few seconds, Mary's life expanded rapidly. An angel with a stunning message: God wanted to live on earth as well as in heaven, God wanted to be born into the line of Mary's own people, the Jews, using her as the bridge between time and eternity, between heaven and earth, between God and people.

Mary asked only one question, halfway through. *She had no husband, how could she have a child?*

This contained everything a woman would need to know. Without a husband, a child was physically impossible. Without a husband, yet pregnant, she would be regarded as a woman without virtue. Without a husband, she would be an unmarried mother, without social position, without financial provision. *Without a husband, how could she have a child?*

Gabriel really answered only one part, that of how Mary could conceive. It was by the power of God, not the power of flesh. Hearing this, Mary was silent. She didn't pursue the other questions, those of her personal, social, financial future.

Mary is a model of simplicity in her love for God. She is a marvel, to those of us who sense the complexities of a situation immediately. She is a person of deep love, reverent faith, unusual trust. Of course she had questions, doubts, fears: but her love was so great that she heard and accepted God's word without becoming confused by the complications.

From Mary we can learn to listen. From Mary we can learn to hear a confusing variety of factors yet ask only the single question that counts. From Mary we can learn to receive *anything* from God. From Mary, we can learn to forsake complication even though the complicating factors are real, and not resolved.

From Mary we can learn to love God simply, giving without reservation, responding without equivocation. From Mary we learn love that says, *You see before you the Lord's servant, let it happen to me as you have said.*

Prayer

Dear God,

Thank you for the simplicity of Mary's love for you, which asks only that which is essential. Thank you for her willingness to serve you with her flesh, to give you her body as well as her heart and mind.

Help me to serve you unreservedly, without the complication I usually find in things. Deliver me from confusion, so my love for you will have full sway in my life. I do love you, Lord, and want to love you more. I pray in the name of Jesus, Mary's gift to me because she gave herself to you. Amen.

Practice

You probably know at least one person whom you automatically 'switch off' when they speak. The next time you're with them, pause, and give them your *full* attention. Listen carefully, trying to hear what they're really saying.

Day 22

Mary Loves God Responsibly

---

*M*ARY *set out at that time and went as quickly as she could into the hill country to a town in Judah. She went into Zechariah's house and greeted Elizabeth. (Luke 1:39–40)*

For what reasons would you go somewhere *immediately*? The death of a relative, the grave illness of a family member, the wedding of a friend? The birth of a child, the unexpected gift of a holiday house, a sudden business crisis? What would cause you to change all your usual plans and rush off?

Would you rearrange your life to receive the counsel of a friend? Would you rearrange all your activities to be comforted in a difficulty, or encouraged by a relative whom you knew would understand *exactly* what you were experiencing?

Whatever her usual life, her regular responsibilities, Mary found it necessary to go her kinswoman Elizabeth. God's word had sought and found her, she had agreed; now she needed the love, the counsel, the assurance of an older woman.

Mary, however faithful, however unique among women on earth, was nevertheless young. An angel had come, God had spoken: she had heard the wisdom of God in a way no other human being had. That was a great responsibility, it could have been an unbearably heavy burden. Mary did not try to bear it alone. She knew she needed help, and she went for it.

Look at the sort of woman Mary chose. Elizabeth was much older, having been married for many years but unable to bear children. Being barren was anathema to her, the worst curse she could have endured on earth: yet still she loved and served God. She was 'upright in the sight of God and impeccably carried out all the commandments and observances of the Lord.' (Luke 1:6)

Elizabeth, then, was a woman of sorrow and faith. She had known deep disappointment, but had still maintained her relationship with God. She had not cursed God, cut God out of her life or refused to serve God.

Secondly, because childbearing was the most important function a woman fulfilled in Jewish society, Elizabeth had suffered socially. She had been gossiped about, her barrenness had been interpreted as a deliberate act of God, who obviously did not consider Elizabeth worthy of children. Elizabeth herself speaks 'of the humiliation I suffered in public.' Yet still she was faithful to God.

Elizabeth was also a kinswoman of Mary's. They didn't see each other often, since they lived a far distance apart, about seventy-five miles. But the cousins probably saw each other regularly at Festivals in Jerusalem.

Further, Elizabeth herself was also expecting a child. Even if she was just six months pregnant to Mary's not-yet-one, still, she would know more about it than Mary did.

Finally, Elizabeth's child was also by the intervention of God. John who became the Baptist was born of his father Zechariah's seed, but the womb which conceived him had been opened by God. Elizabeth had been barren: now she was fruitful. The couple had been painfully childless, longing for children; then God spoke, saying they would have a son, and Elizabeth conceived. There was no doubt as to the miraculous.

Elizabeth then, was the perfect woman for Mary to visit.

But Mary herself faced risks in going. No one really knew she was pregnant. But when she returned after an absence of several months, her child would be obvious. People in Nazareth would assume she'd had an affair while away.

The distance is another factor. Seventy or eighty miles is a substantial journey, particularly in a culture that travels by foot. *Anyone* would need strength and determination to walk that distance, and a pregnant woman would need extra strength, extra determination. And did Mary travel alone? Most unlikely . . . but how did she arrange it? Did her parents help, had she talked with them? Did Joseph help? Did she join a caravan, have a special escort?

Mary also risked her image as a responsible daughter. Her family had neither wealth nor leisure, and Mary's contributions to farming, food preparation, laundering, weaving, cleaning, perhaps child care, would be sorely missed.

Mary, in going to Elizabeth, departed radically from what was expected. She probably looked irresponsible, leaving her home, her family and Joseph, going off to a relative's for an extended visit.

In fact, Mary was responsible in a way that few would ever know. This young woman, entrusted with the secret of God, charged with bearing the Son of God, was mature beyond her years in seeking out the fellowship and counsel, the friendship and support, of an older, wiser woman of faith. Mary cared, gravely and responsibly, for that which God had given her.

Prayer

Lord,
    Help me to get my priorities right.
    Teach me to be fully responsible for the words you've spoken to me, the calling you've given me, the cares you've entrusted to me.
    Help me to ask for help. Show me those people of maturity and faith who can counsel, encourage and guide me. I want to play my part, as Mary did, in bringing

to birth the life of Christ on earth, in my home, my relationships, my area. In Jesus' Name, Amen.

Practice

Offer a portion of time to a family member or friend who usually refuses to spend time on themselves. Clean their kitchen, wash their car, care for their children – find a *practical* way to love and release them.

Day 23

Mary Love God Expectantly

*N*OW *it happened that as soon as Elizabeth heard Mary's greeting, the child leapt in her womb and Elizabeth was filled with the Holy Spirit. She gave a loud cry and said, 'Of all women you are the most blessed, and blessed is the fruit of your womb. Why should I be honoured with a visit from the mother of my Lord? Look, the moment your greeting reached my ears, the child in my womb leapt for joy. Yes, blessed is she who believed that the promise made her by the Lord would be fulfilled.' (Luke 1:40–45)*

Expectancy!

It was in the very air of Judah's hill country. It filled Elizabeth's house, filled the hearts and bodies of both women, filled even the children still unseen, hidden in their mothers' wombs.

Expectancy has a sense of the child-like. An expectant person is somehow wide-eyed, waiting, excited, hopeful. But expectancy goes beyond anticipation. It has more substance than anticipation.

Anticipation has a sense of uncertainty. We think, we hope, we imagine an event will happen, but there is no real proof. It may be scheduled, even arranged – but until it occurs, there's no guarantee that it will.

You might anticipate going to a show, but until you're in your seat, you might or might not get there. You might anticipate an evening with friends, but until the bell rings and they've come in, they might not actually arrive.

Expectation is different. It is concrete. There is proof,

tangible evidence, that what is expected does exist and will occur.

Someone might anticipate a rise in salary after six months of employment. But if it's written in the contract, they will *expect* it. They have evidence, in print, which takes them beyond anticipation and validates hope.

A pregnant woman is more than just anticipatory. She *knows* that she will have a child. She carries a weight, bears a burden, which proves her hope. She also looks forward to being relieved of the weight, to releasing her burden. At a given time, in the fullness of time, she will give birth, and that which presently is seen partially will be seen fully.

An expectant woman is both light-hearted and grave, delighted and serious. She bears life, she also expects life.

There's a close relationship between expectation and the Holy Spirit. The Spirit is the giver of life, in all its forms. The mystery of conception is a co-operation between the Holy Spirit and human beings: God empowers people to create life. The mystery of spiritual birth is a work of the Holy Spirit: God bears us out of our old life, God delivers us from the bondage of our fallen nature.

By the Spirit we are born into God's family, we are made members of the body of Christ. The Spirit gives life, releasing us from the death of physical corruption, leading us into the realm of eternity.

The conception of Jesus was a work of the Spirit. It united spirit and flesh, God and Mary, God and us. This spiritual act took physical form, joining heaven and earth, overwhelming the power of death with the power of life.

This story of two expectant women is full of the Holy Spirit. In them we witness the Spirit's life, the Spirit's work, the Spirit's power and activity.

Mary was entirely expectant. She had heard and

obeyed God, she *expected* God's promise to be fulfilled. She had given herself to God, she *expected* God's salvation to be accomplished. She *expected* to find Elizabeth preparing for motherhood. She *expected* to be welcomed, counselled, encouraged.

Mary was *expecting* God, not just in spiritual terms but in literal ones. She carried in her body the *proof* of God: she was pregnant, she was expecting.

Elizabeth too was expectant. When she heard Mary's voice, she was filled with the Spirit. She was overwhelmed by God's power, God's revelation, God's life, wisdom, knowledge. Elizabeth shouted aloud, in praise and wonder, humility and thanksgiving.

Elizabeth's child, alive, not yet born, secure in the warmth of her womb, was also touched by God. Responding to the move of the Spirit in his mother's life, John too was moved. The baby 'leapt for joy', experiencing even in his primal state the knowledge, the power, the love of God who was Saviour.

Elizabeth realised with prophetic comprehension the wonder and gift of God's salvation: the *blessing*. Mary was blessed, Mary's child was blessed, she and her own child were blessed: and this was only the beginning. The whole *world* was to be blessed.

Elizabeth's final exclamation summarises Mary's extraordinary relationship with God. 'Blessed is she who believed that the promise made her by the Lord would be fulfilled!' The promise Mary heard in hope and accepted in faith was already being fulfilled. Mary was pregnant: she was expectant.

Prayer

Spirit of the living God,
    Fall afresh on me.
    Break me, melt me, mold me, fill me.
Spirit of the living God,
    Fall afresh on me. Amen.

Practice

Who is a friend that always welcomes you warmly, delighted to see you? Say a prayer of thanksgiving for them.

Day 24

Mary Loves God Humbly

---

*A*ND *Mary said,*
'My soul proclaims the greatness of the Lord
and my spirit rejoices in God my Saviour:
because he has looked upon the humiliation of his servant.
Yes, from now onwards all generations will call me blessed,
for the Almighty has done great things for me.' (Luke
1:46–48)

What words come to your mind when you read these words?

     Over/_____
     Up/_____
     Before/_____
     Stop/_____

And when you read these?

     You/_____
     Heaven/_____
     I/_____
     He/_____

Conjunctions and opposites, that's what these are.

Opposites are different, opposites are 'other than', opposites literally oppose.

Conjunctions are the opposite. They show a relationship between, they make a link. There does not have to be disagreement.

Opposites and conjunctions are easily confused. That which is held together can be taken apart; that which is separate can just as easily be fitted together. But whether we perceive an event, or an experience, or life, as opposing or conjoined will depend largely on us.

95

Mary's hymn of praise to God is a series of opposites and conjunctions. But she always holds the balance. She always gets the relationships and responses in just the right order.

Notice that it's filled with 'my's. Yet it's also filled with 'he's. Mary sings God's praises, but she doesn't leave herself out of the song. God is not sovereign and isolated, God is sovereign and involved. God is not withdrawn in heaven, God is active on earth.

Mary's soul proclaims: but it is God's greatness which is praised. Mary's spirit rejoices: but it is in God that she finds joys. Mary is in a humiliating situation: but God sees this. Mary will be blessed by millions of people yet to live: but it is because of what God has done.

Mary does not pit herself against God. She is not angry with God for calling her to such a difficult task. She is humiliated, because all her world thinks she is immoral, but she joins God in his plan, rather than opposing God or asking him to do it differently. Socially she is compromised: but she bears this without rage, rancour or revenge. Mary accepts humiliation humbly.

Nor does Mary inflate herself. It is not she who has done great things, it is the Almighty. Mary doesn't concentrate on herself, although the calling and action of God in her life are *completely* unique. No other woman on earth will have such an opportunity. No other woman will suffer or rejoice as Mary. Yet Mary does not dwell on her chosenness, her favouredness. She dwells on the greatness of God, the saving grace of God, the perception of God, the works of God. Mary accepts her uniqueness humbly.

Oppositely, Mary does not reduce herself. She is not preoccupied with why *she* has this calling, why *she* has been chosen. She does not bewail her inadequacies, cry out that she is unworthy, give all the reasons why she is unable to fulfill God's will. Rather, Mary gives herself fully to doing it well. She makes available to God every natural capacity, giving her body to incarnate God, her soul to proclaim the greatness of God, her spirit to rejoice in God. Mary accepts her competence humbly.

Mary loves God humbly. She does not oppose God or God's ways. She joins herself to God. She does not set herself over or under God. She holds together *heaven* and *earth*, *stop* and *go*, *yes* and *no*. Mary makes *me* and *you* conjunctions, not opposites, in relating to God.

Prayer

Holy Spirit,
Use everything I have, all I am and own, to praise and glorify God. Stop me from exalting or reducing myself, teach me to proclaim God's goodness. Take me closer to Jesus, the Lord of my life. Amen.

Practice

Send a card or note anonymously to someone whom you think is a sort of 'unsung hero', often doing kind deeds but perhaps not always appreciated enough.

Day 25

Mary Loves God Prophetically

'*HOLY is God's name,
and his faithful love extends age after age to those
who fear him.
He has used the power of his arm,
he has routed the arrogant of heart.
He has pulled down princes from their thrones and raised
high the lowly.
He has filled the starving with good things, sent the rich
away empty.
He has come to the help of Israel his servant, mindful of
his faithful love-according to the promise he made to
our ancestors –
of his mercy to Abraham and to his descendants for ever.*'
(Luke 1:49–55)

Mary's praise has changed. Before, it centred on God
and God's actions in her life. Now it has broadened.
Mary has gone from the particular to the universal.

And what a panoramic vision she has! Mary declares
God's action in past, present and future; she describes
God's attitude toward power, pride, oppression, wealth.

Mary exalts in God's personality. God is *holy*, God is
faithfully loving. God is active, *using, routing, pulling
down, raising up, filling, sending away, helping*. God works
in time, his love extending *age after age*, fulfilling promises made *to our ancestors*.

Mary describes God's personal involvement, not only
with herself, but with *all generations*. She specifys God's
care for her people, *Israel, God's servant* and recalls that

it was to *Abram* and then *his descendants* that God would be merciful and pour out blessing.

Mary continues to speak in opposites and conjunctions. This time the opposites are emphasised. God's holiness, faithful love and mercy are his motivating characteristics.

God's power is used to rout the arrogant of heart. Those who possess power and are proud, those who live cut off from God in the strength of their own arms, the provision of their own might, have been displaced. They have been forcibly turned out. Because God is a God of righteousness.

Those who have been in high positions, in places of authority and power, have been brought down. Their kingdoms of deception and illusion have been shattered, they have been removed from their positions of honour and tribute because of their misuse of power. Because God is a God of justice.

Those who have been downtrodden, downcast, oppressed, those who have been in the lowest position: they have been raised and set up high, by God's power and authority. Because God is a God of vindication.

Those who have had nothing, whose very lives have been at risk, those who have ceased to be, because they hadn't even the bread or rice or milk to survive – they have been filled with plenteousness. They have been given all the good things which make strong bones, healthy muscles, alert minds, stable emotions. And those who have feasted, who have eaten richly and well, feeding on the poverty of the oppressed: they have been sent away *empty*. Because God is a God of compassion, a God of generosity.

Mary's words, then, link opposites. Awe/arrogance, princes/lowly, pull down/raise high, fill/empty, starving/rich.

And she uses at least one conjunction. 'God's faithful love extends age after age to those who *fear* God.' What is her meaning? It's to be fully aware of the person in

99

every aspect of their being. To fear God is to acknowledge the whole of God: his life, his commands, his power, strength, authority.

If this is our relationship to God, we are assured of his faithful love, his mercy, his compassion for our humiliation, his faithfulness to our children and their children, his rich provision of everything needed for life.

But, only if we fear God. As Mary did. She accepted the fullness of God deeply, personally. She rejected no part of God or God's word because it didn't fit her hopes or suit her lifestyle. She was completely open to God and God's will, not only for herself, but for her people and the entire world. Mary allowed God to be himself: righteous, just, vindicating, compassionate, generous, faithfully loving, merciful.

People who let God be God are prophetic. They accept, embody, and speak God's word. Jesus, Mary's child, was the enfleshment of that word. He speaks prophetically to us: 'It is not anyone who says to me, "Lord, Lord," who will enter the kingdom of Heaven, but the person who does the will of my Father in heaven.' (Matt. 7:21).

In her personal and prophetic song of praise, Mary makes clear what God's will is. Righteousness, justice, vindication, compassion, generosity, faithful love, mercy. Are they opposites or conjunctions in your life?

Prayer

Lord,

I confess that your ways are not my ways. I love you, but I love other things as well. I believe that I trust you deeply, but I also depend on money, status and power to make my life comfortable. What I possess I don't want to forsake, what I have yet to gain I don't want to forego.

Be compassionate, Lord, and help me. Change me, to be like Mary, to trust you fully. In your Name, Jesus, Amen.

Practice

Get a leaflet and poster about a country suffering from famine or drought, from your church or local Oxfam shop. Read them well, then post them somewhere in your home for ten days. Each time you pass them, say a quick prayer for the situation.

Day 26

Mary Loves God Freely

---

*N*OW *it happened that at this time Ceasar Augustus issued a decree that a census should be made of the whole inhabited world . . . Everyone went to be registered, each to his own town. So Joseph set out from the town of Nazareth in Galilee for Judea, to David's town called Bethlehem, since he was of David's House and line, in order to be registered together with Mary, his betrothed, who was with child. Now it happened that, while they were there, the time came for her to have her child, and she gave birth to a son, her first-born. She wrapped him in swaddling clothes and laid him in a manger because there was no room for them in the living-space. (Luke 2:3–6)*

Why do you want to be loved?

What does being loved mean to you? What do you require, to feel you are loved? What do you ask – not necessarily aloud, but to yourself – of a relationship? What has to happen for you to trust love?

Think for a time, and discover what is important to you about being loved. What are the 'what's, the 'why's, the 'how's of it?

'Unconditional' might describe the kind of love for which we long. Sometimes we are angry, and very unkind – what we want are people who aren't put off by this. Sometimes we are nasty, blatantly selfish – what we hope for are people who will accept us anyway. We shouldn't want them to approve or rationalise away our irresponsibility or immaturity; rather that they will love and respect us despite our sin.

If we've become vulnerable to others, letting them see

the negative as well as positive side of our personality, we want them to be truly trust-worthy. We don't want them to use their 'inside knowledge' of our weaknesses to manipulate us. We don't want to be dependant upon them, or blackmailed emotionally, so that their power over us prevents us growing out of our sinfulness.

We also hope to be loved freely. There are times when we can't keep our word, although we would have sworn we could. There are times when things happen unpredictably, when appointments get confused, when arrangements are muddled, because we didn't really take in what was being said. At these times, when confusion reigns, miscommunication triumphs, and apparent malice surfaces, we want to be loved freely, without condemnation or rejection. We don't want love to depend on our perfection. We don't want love to disappear because of conflict or, even worse, trauma.

It is this kind of love, unconditional, accepting, free, that Mary has for God. Life was certainly not what she would have thought, yet she freely re-adjusted, changed, re-arranged.

Of course she expected to have her baby in Nazareth. It was her home, and a familiar environment always helps with a new, demanding experience. But political events took precedence over Mary's personal life. A census was ordered. As a citizen in an occupied nation, Mary had no choice but to obey the order to return to Joseph's hometown. The ways of the world were more powerful and much larger than Mary's control over her circumstances.

It meant a long, arduous journey, even further than the one to Elizabeth's. And in the *last* weeks of her pregnancy this time. It was so tiring, such a lot of preparation, packing up of clothes and supplies, taking along things for the baby's birth. Then the exhausting travel itself . . .

Upon arrival, Mary found they could not find any place to stay. There was not room in Joseph's family home, nor in a public inn. Only in a manger, a poorly-built shed for animals tacked onto a house. Perhaps it *was* warm. It wouldn't have been clean. And it probably smelled, the strong, clinging, noxious musk of goats, the sweat, hair, straw and dung of sheep.

The scriptures usually tell us what people thought and felt. We learn that they were afraid, or angry, or threatened. But there's no record of Mary's responses to this momentous event in her life. Her first child, a child conceived by God: and nothing happening the way she had thought.

Mary loved God freely. She accepted her circumstances, social, political and personal. She was not *captive* to them, so if there was danger or change was necessary, it was well heeded and action taken. But Mary did not complain. She did not reject the inexplicable hardships life brought her. She trusted God in everything, even in the wearing journey to have her name written in the foreign conqueror's book. Even in the exhausted disappointment that there was no place to stay. Even in the discouraging environment where she had her baby.

Mary didn't demand that God do things her way. She was not conditional in her love for God. She didn't give God a list of requirements as to what she would and wouldn't do, what she could and couldn't manage, what God should and shouldn't do. She loved God in the midst of difficulties, in events that she knew God would not have chosen for her.

This free love is a great gift. It values its recipient. It affirms that whatever has happened, the relationship remains unchanged.

God did not *have* to give Mary what any new mother would have hoped for. Mary was content to cope with change. Mary's love for God was so strong, so sure, that she suffered change and disappointment and still loved God freely.

We want to be loved, we want to be loved unconditionally. God does too.

Prayer

Lord of love,
 Make me more like Mary.

I admire her trust. I am touched by her love for you
and how practically she lived it out. I'm a bit in awe of
her, her stamina, her faithfulness, her ability to cope and
adjust. Use my personality, my situations, my life, to
make me more like her, free to express my love for you.
Amen.

Practice

See how you can help care for and protect children.
Become part of a neighbourhood group, organise a car
pool, walk with them through unsafe areas. Ask at the
local school for more ways.

Day 27

Mary Loves God Patiently

IN the countryside close by there were shepherds out in the fields keeping guard over their sheep during the watches of the night. An angel of the Lord stood over them and the glory of the Lord shone round them. They were terrified, but the angel said, 'Do not be afraid. Look, I bring you news of great joy, a joy to be shared by the whole people. Today in the town of David a Saviour has been born to you; he is Christ the Lord. And here is a sign for you: you will find a baby wrapped in swaddling clothes and lying in a manger.' And all at once with the angel there was a great throng of the hosts of heaven, praising God with the words:

> *Glory to God in the highest heaven,*
> *and on earth peace for those he favours.*

So the shepherds hurried away and found Mary and Joseph, and the baby lying in the manger. When they saw the child they repeated what they had been told about him, and everyone who heard it was astonished at what the shepherds said to them. As for Mary, she treasured all these things and pondered them in her heart. (Luke 2:8–14, 16–19)

In the Christian life there is much waiting, God speaks, but it may be months or years before the promised fruit appears. God speaks, but decades may pass before the word is fulfilled.

Waiting isn't easy. At first we don't mind too much, but after a fairly short time we find we mind a great deal. We are not as prepared as we'd thought to walk rather than run, to sit rather than walk, to kneel rather than sit. Waiting stirs within us all that is anxious. Waiting reveals our pockets of restlessness and fear, our crevices of anger and resentment. Waiting unearths all that is not patient.

Mary waited patiently with God. She waited before God, receiving God's word, not understanding, still believing.

She was as astonished as Joseph when the shepherds arrived, filled with gabble and wonder, spilling out their stunning experience.

Yet their story had a familiar ring. Again there was an angel, innumerable angels, in fact. Again there was heavenly revelation, God's announcing his intention of universal salvation. Again there was prophetic content, linking past, present and future. Again there was proof in a tangible sign, a child. Just as Gabriel had told Mary that Elisabeth was pregnant, and she had found it so, these angels told the shepherds that a child had been born: and it was so.

Mary *was* as astonished as Joseph to hear God's truth from complete strangers. They'd never met these people, the shepherds couldn't possibly have known about them or their newborn son. Yet here they were, every word echoing what they'd heard from God months before.

Mary's response went beyond her initial astonishment. Mary treasured and pondered these prophetic mysteries. She held them close, remembering them, caring for them, respecting and honouring them. Mary *treasured* what the shepherds said, making it a source of wealth and riches. They were transformed from mere words or strange story into objects of immense value.

But these sacred objects were not placed in a case and stared at. Mary pondered them in her *heart*. They went straight to the centre of her being. There they stayed, cared for, tended to, puzzled over, meditated upon. They were living words, causing her to question, reflect.

Mary waited, not just a night or a month, but years. Mary waited patiently upon God, treasuring, pondering, until God's plan was accomplished before her and all the world. This was a plan *of great joy to be shared by all the people*. Mary bore it painfully but patiently, waiting for God to do what had been promised.

Prayer

Breathe on me, Breath of God,
  Until my heart is pure,
  Until with you I will one will, to do and to endure.
    Amen.

(E. Hatch)

Practice

Find an object you value, perhaps a favourite pen, a small vase, a necklace, a book, a photograph. Keep it in plain sight for a few days, treasuring it, then give it away. If you find this hard to do, talk to the Lord about your feelings.

Day 28

Mary Loves God Properly

*W*HEN *the eighth day came and the child was to be circumcised, they gave him the name Jesus, the name the angel had given him before his conception. And when the day came for them to be purified in keeping with the Law of Moses, they took him up to Jerusalem to present him to the Lord – observing what is written in the Law of the Lord: Every first-born male must be consecrated to the Lord – and also to offer in sacrifice, in accordance with what is prescribed in the Law of the Lord, a pair of turtledoves or two young pigeons. (Luke 2:21–24)*

It wouldn't have been hard for Mary to become isolated from the religious institution of her time. Her hearing of God was unusual. Her experiences with God were unparalled. God's actions in her life were unprecedented. Mary easily could have become a law unto herself.

Instead, she fulfilled the obligations enjoined upon her by Jewish tradition. All children were to be circumcised, so Jesus was, his flesh marked for God. All women were to be purified after childbirth; Mary offered herself for the rites. She also presented Jesus in the Temple, a public admission that one's child was given back to God. This ceremony wasn't even required. It was optional, left to the parents' discretion. Mary and Joseph chose it.

Mary's love for God is beautiful in its attitude. She loved God properly, fulfilling all her tradition required, and more. She didn't claim that the work of the Spirit exempted her from the usual order. Neither, because of her commitment to the tradition, did she deny the uniqueness of the Spirit's work. For instance, she named her child *Jesus*, the name spoken by God. She didn't give him a family name, as would have been expected.

Mary held together what we are tempted to take apart as waves of renewal sweep over Christendom. Many Christians today vie with each other, claiming tradition against the work of the Spirit, claiming the renewal of the Spirit against the institution.

The 'side' taken usually depends on personal experience. If you have experienced God powerfully by the Spirit, and your church refuses to listen to you, refuses to accept you, refuses to do more than give an institutional nod in your direction, aren't you justified in leaving to establish a new order? Mustn't you create *new* traditions, new groupings, to compensate for the lacks in the old?

What if you have faithfully served God in your local church, praying quietly, singing the old hymns regularly, caring for the needy, organising the Harvest Festivals and the Childrens' Carol Service, year in, year out? Why should you be displaced, challenged, by people who want to *change* everything? Change the music, change the prayers, change the pews, change the words, change the building . . . everything will be lost.

Or perhaps you've never had much to do with the church. You've always been on the edge, loving and serving God in your own way. You don't feel comfortable with others, or don't like all that dancing, or feel that children are too loud or too quiet. It's easier just to get on with things, and not bother about the church.

Whatever our experience, we can learn from Mary. She respected the traditions, going beyond the requirements; she also respected the Spirit's spontaneity, following obediently. She did not divide God's word and God's work, she did not reject the past because of the present, nor prevent the future because of the past. Mary did not hold her experience with God as a standard, neither did she forsake it.

Mary's willingness to hold past and present together

bore fruit for the future. There was corruption in the religious establishment of her time, just as history and life show there is corruption in ours. There was also grace and truth in the traditional order, and so is there in ours. As with Mary, we should respect both tradition and Spirit. Let us name the illness and encourage the health.

Mary showed by her actions the love in her heart. Her heart was perfect before God.

For us, the question is not so much *what* we do as *why* and *how* we do it. What motivates you? What is in your heart? Bitterness, hurt and anger, or love, patience, compassion? If your heart is pure, then you are free to choose whatever God says, or whatever you desire. There doesn't have to be a right and a wrong, a should or an ought. But if your heart is not pure, you will have your bitterness and rage wherever you go, wherever you stay. They will be wherever you are. You will never be able to love God properly.

Prayer

Lord,

Create a clean heart in me, put into me a new and constant spirit. Don't banish me from your presence, don't deprive me of your Holy Spirit.

Be my saviour again, renew my joy, keep my spirit steady and willing. Amen. (David, Psalm 51)

Practice

Write down the names of three people you dislike or find it hard to get on with. Sit quietly for a few minutes, then ask God to show you why it's hard for you to love these people. Pray that you'll be changed, then imagine each of them and pray for them, one by one.

Day 29

Mary Loves God Sacrificially

. . . *A*ND *also to offer in sacrifice, in accordance with what is prescribed in the Law of the Lord, a pair of turtledoves or two young pigeons.* (Luke 2:24)

What do you count your most valued possessions? What are your most important gifts, your most precious investments?

Is God pleased with these? Does God value them? Should you offer them to God? Would God want them?

Can you actually give God *anything*? Doesn't God already possess everything, heaven, the universe, all power, authority, wisdom and glory? Is it *foolishness* to give God things, an absurdity?

These aren't new questions. For thousands of years people have wondered what to give God. People who don't know God, who have heard only tales or rumours, sometimes give what they hold most dear. Otherwise, God might take it from them . . .

Even the Israelites, God's own people, were sometimes unsure what to give God. 'With what shall I enter the Lord's presence and bow down before God All-High? Shall I enter with burnt offerings, with calves one year old? Will God be pleased with rams by the thousand, with ten thousand streams of oil? Shall I offer my eldest son for my wrong-doing, the child of my own body for my sin?' (Micah 6:6–7)

Mary faced many temptations about giving to God.

Initially, there was the required sacrifice. The offering Mary and Joseph made, 'two pigeons or a pair of turtle-doves', however poetic it sounds to our imaginations,

112

was the offering given by the poor. These birds were cheap and common, and satisfied one's obligation to God.

Mary could have been ashamed of this offering. After all, she had just borne the Son of God. The *only* Son of God. The child who would become the man to liberate his country. A king, an heir of God. How could such a one be presented with such a *poor* offering? The sacrifice certainly wouldn't honour the stature of the person it represented; nor, possibly, would it impress God much. Was it insulting God, to give so little in the light of who Jesus was?

Alternatively, Mary could have compared the *greatness* of God's action, in becoming incarnate as a human, with the *insignificance* of the Law's requirements, the gift of two little birds. Surely, with this great action, with this astounding plan of universal reconciliation, God had moved beyond the original structures.

Again, Mary could have recalled her own sacrifice, giving her life, her body, her reputation, her future; and concluded that already she had given God far more than was expected.

We have the same temptations. If you live a life of full-time ministry, haven't you already given God everything? Surely you are exempt from offering a tithe of your money or support. Why, that would actually be a *further* contribution deducted from the fullness of what you've already given.

If you work for peace and justice, struggling for those less fortunate, writing, speaking and campaigning for those denied freedom, employment, economy and education, haven't you already given yourself fully to the Gospel? Are there other offerings God could want? Could God speak to you about prayer, asking you to spend one-tenth or even one-quarter of your time in prayer, rather than action, for these concerns?

What if you have no money? What if your income is so reduced or non-existent, or your financial commitments so indebted, that you have nothing to give? Could time become your sacrifice? Could you work for others, who are also unemployed – using your now redundant training? Could you care for the sick or shop regularly for the elderly, could you coach the young, in sport or maths or reading?

Mary was both ordinary and extraordinary. Either could have tempted her, to excuse herself from what God required.

Her ordinariness, her regular responsibilities and commitments, could have convinced her that sacrifice was impossible. After all, she was a new wife, a young mother, a home-maker with ever re-occuring responsibilities. There was too much to do, too much to get used to, too much daily life, to be able to sacrifice to God.

Her extraordinariness, alternatively, could have set her apart from everyone else. God had given her an immense mission and responsibility, and she *wasn't* like everyone else. Why should she be subject to the religious rules that governed others? She was unique, and different.

Mary survived all these temptations. She offered the two tiny birds, the sacrifice of the poor.

Prayer

Lord Jesus,

In your life I see your parents' influence. God your Father gave you freely to the world, so you could live with us in flesh. Mary your mother gave herself freely to God, offering her whole life in service. Joseph adopted you on earth, giving freely the protection, shelter and home which you needed.

Thank you, Lord, for making me a member of your family. Perfect me by your Spirit, so I can give freely to you and others. Amen.

Practice

Read again the considerations above. Select the area *most* applicable, then decide or discuss a change. Plan how to implement it.

Day 30

Mary Loves God Courageously

---

*N*OW *in Jerusalem there was a man named Simeon,
he was an upright and devout man; he looked
forward to the restoration of Israel and the Holy Spirit
rested on him. It had been revealed to him by the Holy
Spirit that he would not see death until he had set eyes on
the Christ of the Lord.*

*Prompted by the Spirit he came to the Temple; and when
the parents brought in the child Jesus for him to do what
the Law required, he took him into his arms and blessed
God; and he said, 'Now, Master, you are letting your
servant go in peace as you promised; for my eyes have seen
the salvation which you have made ready in the sight of
the nations; a light of revelation for the Gentiles and glory
for your people Israel.'*

*As the child's father and mother were wondering at the
things that were being said about him, Simeon blessed
them and said to Mary his mother, 'Look, he is destined
for the fall and for the rise of many in Israel, destined to
be a sign that is opposed – and a sword will pierce your
soul too – so that the secret thoughts of many may be laid
bare.' (Luke 2:25–35)*

Such a lot had happened in Mary's life in so little time.
God had sent an angel, she had conceived by the Spirit,
Elisabeth had produced a child. There'd been the sorting
out with Joseph of her pregnancy, the trek to Bethlehem
for the census, Jesus' birth in a stable, the arrival of
unknown people, shepherds and kings or wise men,
filled with still more tales of angels, stars, heavenly kings,

earthly kings. In less than a year, *all* of life changed, everything turned upside down and around.

Now, meeting Simeon in the Temple at Jesus' presentation. Yet another stranger, whose life was somehow interwoven with hers. Yet another person who looked upon her child and spoke mysteries. Yet another servant of God, led by the Spirit, who prophesied her son's calling and future.

Who was Simeon, Mary and Joseph wondered. How could he say these things? Did he know their meaning? Did they? Were they supposed to?

Did Mary and Joseph now have enough pieces of the puzzle to make a recognisable picture, or were they still largely ignorant? Did they know yet what God would do through this extraordinary child whose very father was God?

Mary was wondering and preoccupied, and listening further when suddenly, this old holy man spoke not just of her child's future but of her own as well.

'And a sword will pierce your soul, too' he told her.

What could this mean?

Being pierced in the flesh by a sword was understandable. A terrible thought, a horribly cruel experience, but understandable. But to be pierced in one's *soul*? By a *sword*?

The spectre of physical pain is frightening. We can't predict that we would stay steadfast and remain loyal to our faith or country or cause, if we were tormented bodily for it. How much more or less frightening is the possibility of emotional torment?

Could we endure verbal threats and lies, wicked mockery, barbarous insults? Could we stay sane if our imaginations were enflamed to envision our families abused or killed? Could we survive the turmoil of uncertainty if we saw husband or brother or father taken by armed captors who are silent about why or where, how long or if ever? Could we cope if someone we respected in Christ spoke confusing but serious and stark words about our future?

These were the questions Mary faced. What was meant, how would it happen, what would happen?

And there was no answer. Not in that moment, nor in any other record in the scriptures. It's possible that the Spirit revealed God's meaning to Mary personally, but we don't know that. All we know is that she heard a personal prophecy which was not interpreted further.

Mary was a courageous woman. She was young in years but mature in virtues. She was chosen by God for an honoured but confusing and incredibly hard task, and she fulfilled it courageously.

Courage is not often mentioned in our age. Historically, courage is related almost exclusively to military exploits or humanitarian heroism. The first are no longer cloaked in glamorous mystique, the latter aren't always known. But courage is a significant virtue, and of great importance for the Christian.

Mary is courageous because she embraced suffering boldly. She had already suffered, in bringing God's child into the world. Now, in meeting Simeon, she learned there was still more suffering ahead. Trials were waiting. And not small ones, but ones of such import that this man of God was informing her directly.

Mary's future was irrevocably prophesied. She would feel the pains of these trials, in her mind, her feelings, her will. Her very soul would be pierced – cut through, sliced open. This piercing would be so severe it was described by a *weapon*, a sword.

Many Christians today feel this piercing of their soul. Some are parents, when they learn that their unborn child will be deformed or debilitated. Some are Latin American families, as they watch their members taken from them by force. Some are peace-makers, who see distorted edited versions of their protests on television, or read in the papers the things they never said. Others are prophets, who fight with word and will for racial justice but refuse violent means; or preachers, who dare to insist that money should be used for food and work, not bombs.

It takes not just courage but great courage to be an active Christian in the world. It means loving as Mary did, loving God, loving God's word, loving God's ways. It means enduring courageously, trusting God completely. It means waiting for the sword that will surely come.

Prayer

Lord,

I pray that you will strengthen me so I have the confidence of my convictions.

Thank you for Simeon, upright and devout, who spoke courageously your Spirit's word. Thank you for Mary, firm and true, who lived courageously through doubt and sorrow. Thank you for your saints now, who courageously proclaim your truth, justice and mercy.

Make me upright, devout and courageous, too, a witness for your Kingdom. Amen.

Practice

Choose a topic of current social concern, such as right-to-life issues, famine in the Third World, political and religious conflict in Eastern Europe, child abuse, nuclear weapons – something that you don't really know much about. For two weeks, watch any television programmes, listen to any radio programmes, read any newspaper or magazine articles on your subject, that you can. Tell others you're doing it, so they can help you find programmes or information.

PART FOUR:

SAUL SERVES GOD
BOOK OF ACTS

Day 31

Saul Serves God with Pride

'**Y**OU stubborn people,' Stephen continued, 'with uncircumcised hearts and ears. You are always resisting the Holy Spirit, just as your ancestors used to do. Can you name a single prophet your ancestors never persecuted? They killed those who foretold the coming of the Upright One, and now you have become his betrayers, his murderers. In spite of being given the Law through angels, you have not kept it.'

They were infuriated when they heard this, and ground their teeth at him . . . All of the members of the Council shouted out and stopped their ears with their hands; then they made a concerted rush at him, thrust him out of the city and stoned him. The witnesses put down their clothes at the feet of a young man called Saul. Saul approved the killing. (Acts 7:51–54, 57–59, 8:1)

Would Saul have recognised himself in Stephen's description? Would we recognise ourselves?

Probably not, in either case. But we might recognise Saul.

Not for a minute would Saul have thought he was *resisting the Spirit*. He was sure he was preserving the work of the Spirit, the Law which bound the Jews to God and each other. It was Stephen, the rebel, the deceived, who was undoing God's work.

Saul did not consider himself *stubborn*, he was stead-fast. He would endure, persevering to the end, defending the established religious order. The people, the faith, the nation must be protected from demented sectarians who destroy tradition, defame truth.

Saul was convinced he was not *uncircumcised of heart or ear*. His body had been circumcised, according to the Law; how dare this misguided man claim his spirit and soul were any less touched by God. Of course Saul's heart was righteous, his ears able to hear God's truth! He'd spent years studying the Law, as a Pharisee he kept it meticulously.

And likening them to their *ancestors*! Those forebears had been flagrantly sinful. They'd broken the Law, they'd been cunning and deceitful in their dealings, they'd blatantly worshipped false gods and sacrificed to idols. There was no comparison between their religious infidelity and upright Jews. These people Stephen accused were staunchly faithful, scrupulously obeying every phrase, every command of the Law.

Stephen was a foolish upstart, and more than foolish, inflammatory. He would pay for this with his blood. And that would be righteous in God's sight, for the Law required that blasphemers be stoned.

Saul, with the others, gave full vent to anger. He rejected Stephen's words, he witnessed Stephen's slaughter. *Saul approved Stephen's killing*.

Our anger too can approve violence and make us agreeable witnesses to death. But it's hard to recognise in ourselves.

Think of *our* 'religious establishment'. It's even more fragmented than Saul's.

If primarily evangelical, are you so preoccupied with personal holiness, personal morality, personal witness, that you don't see the world beyond the circle cast by your 'little light'? Do you judge God's work by defined doctrines, by standardised dogmas? Do you *thrust out of the city and stone* those who can't run your personal gauntlet of witness, declaration and good works?

If you think yourself 'traditional', are you self-congratulatory that you're holding out against all the odds? The needlework is safely organised, the threat of leather or plastic kneelers once again averted. The Flower Rota is finally filled, though most of the parish live on an estate with 46% unemployed, where families struggle to buy food and flowers are from another world. Did you *grind your teeth* during the discussions of 'Neighbourhood Groups', when people would have met twice monthly for supper and personal prayer in each others' homes? Thank God the decision wasn't taken, and midweek meetings will still be confined to Lent!

If charismatic, are you *infuriated* by those who refuse to realise that God doesn't live in a museum, those who reject the prophetic, those who persecute what they don't understand and won't learn about?

If you believe God has 'a preference for the poor', and that the Gospel is God's testament of concern for the underdog, you're especially aware of governmental misuse of power and money. Millions of pounds and dollars are spent yearly, on missiles which become obsolete before completion; stockpiled weapons devour money which could have been spent nationally on homes, jobs, education and the arts, and internationally on restructuring economic systems which prevent two-thirds of the world from having enough food. Are you as aware of God's power as of the human misuse of power? Do you know the God who intervenes, heals, changes, convicts? Can you care for the wealthy neurotic widow as well as the deserted single-parent family? Can you look with eyes of compassion, rather than disgust, on those who link national security and arms, God and the military?

Like Saul, do we recognise the sins of others but

fail to see our own? Are we *breathing murderous threats*, dividing still further the body of Christ? Do we *shout at the truth*, have we *stopped our ears* from hearing the gospel command to love? Do we make a *concerted rush* at those who are different, those we don't understand, those we dislike?

Do we reject and stone others? Not directly, of course, not *real* murder. But slaughter nonetheless. Personally, socially, attitudinally, spiritually.

Are you resisting the Holy Spirit, just as your ancestors used to do?

Prayer

Lord Jesus,

Help me live a life worthy of the vocation to which you've called me. Teach me how, with all humility and gentleness, with patience, I can support all other Christians in love. I want to learn to take every care to preserve the unity of the Spirit by the peace which binds us together. Amen. (Adapted from Paul, Ephesians 4)

Practice

Be honest about your prejudices. Ask the Holy Spirit to widen your heart and open your mind. When people or issues provoke you, expect the Holy Spirit to lead you into repentance. Don't resist change when it comes to you.

Day 32

Saul Serves God with Presumption

SAUL began doing great harm to the church; he went from house to house arresting both men and women and sending them to prison. . . . Meanwhile Saul was still breathing threats to slaughter the Lord's disciples. He went to the high priest and asked for letters addressed to the synagogues in Damascus, that would authorise him to arrest and take to Jerusalem any followers of the Way, men or women, that he might find. (Acts 8:3, 9:1–2)

Saul was a great man, capable of great things. He was one of an elite, a man with a distinctive background and distinguished qualifications.

He was a person of great privilege. He had been raised in a stable Hebrew home by parents who were both diligent and faithful. His unusually high intelligence had been heightened by an excellent education. He was well-travelled, fluent in several languages and had trained under Gamaliel, an impressive, respected rabbi. He'd been well-prepared for a privileged, successful, religious career.

Saul had great gifts. His writings reveal a brilliant legal mind. But he could abandon logic when necessary, to draw out the true meaning of a law, custom or tradition. He was a creative scholar, an original thinker. He used his learning as a foundation, raising upon it structures of unique perception, fresh insight, inspired interpretation.

Other gifts were outstanding. Saul was capable of great devotion, tireless action, impassioned determination. If a cause qualified for his attention, he gave it wholly.

Completely single-minded, nothing deterred him once he had set a goal.

Saul had great power. He was 'an inside man', with immediate access to the religious authority and power of Israel. Jewish rights protected both individual and community: few people could have gone 'from house to house, arresting both men and women and sending them to prison', as Saul did. He must have been extremely convincing in the case he presented to his religious colleagues.

Great political influence was also Saul's. Not only was he Hebrew, he was also a Roman citizen. His citizenship was neither honorary nor acquired, bought by service or cash; it was the genuine article, elite and envied. Saul was a natural born Roman.

This made him privileged in both states. Rome had mastered the art of 'conquering brutally and ruling pacifically': nations could maintain their own traditions, managing their own affairs, as long as they acknowledged Caesar as Lord and Rome as their authority. But the peace in Israel was always uneasy, for Jewish lip-service bordered on insubordination.

Saul had a double access possessed by few. He was equally privileged in both cultures. He shared a common history, tradition and faith with the Jews, he shared birthright, privilege and position with the Romans, the most powerful people in the world.

Saul was great in one other way than privilege, gifts, power, influence. Saul was greatly deceived. For all his faith, for all his action, he was completely out of touch with God.

Saul was not serving God, he was serving his own ambitions. Saul was not defending God, he was defending his own prejudices. Saul wasn't accomplishing the works of God, he was hindering and destroying them.

Saul had great gifts and he used them wrongly. He had great power and authority and used it badly. He had great influence and used it shamefully. He set himself up as God's protector, then judged, condemned, humiliated and controlled. Saul determined what was good or bad, godly or sinful; he himself decided what was meant by God's word and had people maltreated accordingly. Because of the authority he wielded, people were arrested, abducted, imprisoned and killed.

Saul thought his greatness was serving God. But it wasn't. It served his deception, his idea of duty.

Prayer

Jesus,

I know that in certain areas I am great. You have given me great gifts, or great love, or a great desire to follow you. I also know that I have great weaknesses, great failings. I confess both to you, what is good and what is bad, what is lovely and what is ugly. Please take both. Use the first to God's greater glory; refine and remove the other, so I can be a living witness of your mercy. Amen.

Practice

Think of the most presumptuous person you know. What is it about them that irritates you so? How are you different? Are you really?

Day 33

Saul Serves God with Helplessness

*I*T happened that while he was travelling to Damascus
and approaching the city, suddenly a light from heaven
shone all round him. He fell to the ground, and then he
heard a voice saying, 'Saul, Saul, why are you persecuting
me?' 'Who are you, Lord?' he asked, and the answer came,
'I am Jesus, whom you are persecuting. Get up and go
into the city, and you will be told what you are to do.' The
men travelling with Saul stood there speechless, for though
they had heard the voice they could see no one. Saul got
up from the ground, but when he opened his eyes he could
see nothing at all, and they had to lead him into Damascus
by the hand. For three days he was without his sight and
took neither food nor drink.

There was a disciple in Damascus called Ananias, and
he had a vision in which the Lord said to him, 'Ananias!'
When he replied, 'Here I am, Lord,' the Lord said, 'Get
up and go to Straight Street and ask at the house of Judas
for someone called Saul, who comes from Tarsus. At this
moment he is praying and has seen a man called Ananias
coming in and laying hands on him to give him back his
sight.' (Acts 9:3–12)

Relax for a moment. Take a deep breath, close your eyes,
blow out the air. Rest silently, gathering your thoughts.

Reflect on your life for a few minutes. In what areas
do you feel most in charge? Where are you most
powerful, most capable?

What are the areas in which you feel powerless? You
have to implement someone else's ideas or are limited
by another's attitude. You feel prevented, helpless.

Are you resolved about these latter? Do they irritate you, do they cause friction and conflict? Are you trapped?

Perhaps as the only son, you must manage your aging mother's financial matters. But she has always been a controlling person, and won't give you all the information you need. So you have the responsibility but not the facts which facilitate. Or maybe your daughter is living with a man, a situation which saddens you but enrages your husband. His anger is so great that he will neither speak to her nor visit her. Or, perhaps you've just bought your first house, and needed someone to share with you. Friends of the family suggested their youngest child, but only after she'd moved in did you discover she is a secret drug user.

These are situations of helplessness. Not only are we caught and pained, but it's almost impossible to feel that we are serving God in them. We aren't in charge, we don't like what's happening, we don't know how to reconcile reality with our intentions or hopes.

This was Saul's situation. He had left Jerusalem fully in charge, energised by his mission, empowered with authority for his personal crusade: he arrived in Damascus blind, stumbling, unable to eat or drink.

He was reduced from someone who could accomplish whatever he wanted to someone who could only hobble, who saw only darkness, who was so shaken that he could not function normally at all.

It was in this state that Saul served God. He was reduced to dependence, his great powers were useless, he was face to face with God's purposes, not his own, and blinded by the vision.

Saul could do only one thing: pray. He could only sit before God, wait upon God, listen to God.

In that helplessness, Saul found God and power in a new way. When 'reduced' to prayer, he experienced grace and communication he'd never known. God spoke

129

through a vision: God sent a brother, to release Saul from his powerful helplessness.

Helplessness does not have to be hopeless. The gift of prayer will help us, support us, encourage us, reveal God's provision to us.

In your situations of bewildered impotence, use this great gift of prayer. When you can do nothing to break through tyranny, to bring people back together, to solve immediately a grave dilemma, sit before God, blind and helpless like Saul, and pray.

If you do, regularly seeking God's help in these hopeless human affairs, you will be surprised at the results. You will probably discover a deep reservoir of despair, previously well-hidden. You might quickly become terribly bored, then furiously bored. You will resent the time and effort you must give. You will feel God is cruel, callously abandoning you and people you love. You will be infuriated that you must be so involved, wondering why, if God's so loving and powerful, he's so uncaring and powerless.

If you persevere through these initial stages, you will break into a deeper, new relationship with God. Your weeping will be compassionate instead of self-pitying, your intercession will serve God and the situation instead of your self-will and frustration.

Sometimes one doesn't face these agonies. Sometimes only one or two periods of prayer produce a remarkable change. Turns untwist, knots unslip, people about-face. But more frequently, we will have, comparable to Saul, 'three days without sight and neither food nor drink'. We won't necessarily be released quickly from our helplessness. It might take weeks, or months, sometimes even years.

But God *will* provide. He'll give a vision, empower a change, send a friend. You will be released from your helplessness, you will know the Spirit's power.

Prayer

Lord Jesus,

Your ways with Saul were wonderful. You spoke into his darkness, you gave vision despite his blindness.

Speak to me, Lord, saving me from my errors, releasing me from my helplessness. Teach me to pray. Teach me to wait: shed light, give sight. Amen.

Practice

Observe the people in your local fellowship. Are there any who are willing but seem uncertain what to do or how to become more involved? Get to know them, invite them to join you in one or two of your activities.

Day 34

Saul Serves God without Reservation

---

*T*HE Lord said to Ananias, 'Get up and go to Straight
Street and ask at the house of Judas for someone
called Saul, who comes from Tarsus. At this moment he is
praying, and has seen a man called Ananias coming in
and laying hands on him to give him back his sight.'
But in response, Ananias said, 'Lord, I have heard from
many people about this man and all the harm he has been
doing to your holy people in Jerusalem. He has come here
with a warrant from the chief priests to arrest everybody
who invokes your name.' The Lord replied, 'Go, for this
man is my chosen instrument to bring my name before
gentiles and kings and before the people of Israel; I myself
will show him how much he must suffer for my name.'
(Acts 9:11–17)

Saul's repentance was as great as his deception. And
though his deception lasted only a short while, his unreserved service to God lasted the whole of his life.

Saul had always been an extremist. Whatever he
believed, whatever he committed himself to, he did unreservedly. If he was going to teach, then he would be a
brilliant teacher, and a perfectionist. If he was going
to obey the Law of God, then he would exemplary in
obedience, and a Pharisee. If he was going to protect
the faith, then he would be a rigorous defender, and a
persecutor. Similarly, when he was converted to Christ,
he was the most extreme of all converts, unparalled in
service, fidelity and devotion.

From the Damascus road on, Saul was *never* the same.
God's mercy reached out to Saul, as he travelled from

Jerusalem on his blood hunt. God saved Saul, from his prejudice, his ignorance, his abuse of power and blood-guilt. On the Damascus road, Jesus halted Saul, saving him from his legalism and destructiveness. The Spirit of God humbled Saul, striking him to the ground, blinding him with a radiance unknown on earth.

Then God gave him two things, a vision and a friend. In Jesus' name, Ananias delivered Saul from his blindness and baptised him into new life.

Saul was made powerless, struck sightless and humbled, then befriended, restored, empowered. This series of events was so overwhelming that he never recovered. Saul's experience of Jesus was so personal, so direct, so unassailable, he never again questioned Jesus' relationship to God, or God's salvation through Christ. Nor did he question his own relationship to Jesus, or the re-dedication of his life, from servant of the Law to slave of Christ. From the Damascus road on, Saul was unquestioning, unrelenting, unreserved in living out his commitment to Christ.

This unreserved service cost him dearly. Never again would he live the comfortable life of a Pharisee, studying for hours in pleasant rooms, having stimulating theor-etical discussions with other scholars, living a pre-sched-uled life of worship, study and sacrifice. Never again was Saul secure as the well-born, well-educated successful young protegee of the Sanhedrin. He was suspect, undesirable, unacceptable. He who had set out enflamed, to quench the rebellion which threatened the Jewish establishment, had become the greatest rebel of them all.

From the Damascus road on, Saul's life was erratic and unpredictable. It was pushed to the edge, threatened by death. It was studded with theological arguments that made the difference between eternal life and death for the participants. Saul lived in on-going risk, without any of the guarantees we feel we need.

Saul served God *without reservation*. Without any prearrangements, that there would be a home, a meal or even a shelter. Without any reliable 'calling ahead', so that the hope of warmth and rest could be held against the stress of escaping hostile Jews or angry Gentiles. Without any preparations or reception committees, without any assurance that the place he was going next would offer a welcome.

Saul did without many pleasures and privileges. He had no home but settled temporarily in several countries; he had no family but was father to thousands of children in Christ; he had no consistent co-worker, but was joined randomly by people whom the Spirit singled out or who offered themselves short-term for specific missions.

Saul, feeling cornered because he was being compared to others, once catalogued his fortunes and misfortunes as the resolute, unreserved servant of Christ. 'I have done more work, I have been in prison more, I have been flogged more severely, many times exposed to death. Five times I have been given the thirty-nine lashes by the Jews; three times I have been beaten with sticks; once I was stoned; three times I have been shipwrecked, and once I have been in the open sea for a night and a day; continually travelling, I have been in danger from my own people and in danger from the Gentiles, in danger in the towns and in danger in the open country, in danger at sea and in danger from people masquerading as brothers; I have worked with unsparing energy, for many nights without sleep; I have been hungry and thirsty, and often altogether without food or drink; I have been cold and lacked clothing. And, besides all the external things, there is, day in day out, the pressure on me of my anxiety for all the churches. If anyone weakens, I am weakened as well; and when anyone is made to fall, I burn in agony myself.' (2 Cor. 11:23–29)

The cost of Saul's conversion was high. God paid a high price, through the suffering of Jesus and the persecution of Saul's innocent victims; Saul paid a high price, through his unfailing sacrifice of his life, his giftedness, his greatness. God knew how painful Saul's service would be, and how deeply Saul's love for Christ would stir him. *I myself will show him*, God said to Ananias, *how much he must suffer for my name.*

Prayer

Lord Jesus,

I long to know your love as surely as Saul did. I want to be changed by you, now and in the years to come, so that my love is unqualified and my service unreserved.

I pray this for the glory of God, and with thanksgiving for Saul, who loved so deeply, served so fully, gave so wholly. Amen.

Practice

Which family member gives lots of time to putting others' needs first? Write or ring them, to say you appreciate their sacrifices.

Day 35

Saul Serves God with Power

'*THEN Ananias went. He entered the house, and laid his hands on Saul and said, 'Brother Saul, I have been sent by the Lord Jesus, who appeared to you on your way here, so that you may recover your sight and be filled with the Holy Spirit.' It was as though scales fell away from his eyes and immediately he was able to see again. So he got up and was baptised, and after taking some food he regained his strength.*

After he had spent only a few days with the disciples in Damascus, he began preaching in the synagogues, 'Jesus is the Son of God.' All his hearers were amazed, and said, 'Surely, this is the man who did such damage in Jerusalem to the people who invoke this name, and who came here for the sole purpose of arresting them to have them tried by the chief priests?'

Saul's power increased steadily, and he was able to throw the Jewish colony at Damascus into complete confusion by the way he demonstrated that Jesus was the Christ.' (Acts 9:17–22)

The Holy Spirit is the power of God to change our lives. The work of the Spirit is consistent, continual and comprehensive. The Spirit cleanses us, purifys us, restores us, heals us.

The Spirit releases us from the *power* of the fear of death. The Spirit changes our habits of fear, manipulation, self-centredness. Sometimes the Spirit must work slowly over a period of years to free us from familiar sins and comforts. Other times the Spirit moves very quickly, releasing us miraculously and immediately from ancient bondages.

We rarely know how God will work with any given part of our broken humanity. To be redeemed from the fall of Adam – from the tyranny of our materialism, from our dependence upon that which we can touch, see, control – is an overwhelming task. Only God could attempt it, only God can accomplish it.

God knows how much we can endure at any point. God knows our frailty as well as our strength, God respects and is mindful of our limits. This is why we 'work out our salvation in fear and trembling.' Redemption is an on-going process, occurring in time, taking time. We are often impatient: it is God who knows the depth of our brokenness, and the care which must be taken in restoring us to be the people he always intended.

Saul's life is a witness to the power of the Spirit of God. The Spirit turned Saul's life completely around, and Saul followed. The Spirit sat Saul down, and Saul remained. The Spirit spoke to another Christian, and Saul received. The Spirit immersed Saul's life in God's own life, baptising him through the touch of another person: and Saul was empowered. Empowered to repent: to stay turned around. Empowered to preach, to declare boldly what before he had persecuted. Empowered to teach and discuss, to demonstrate and prove the Lordship of the Christ he had rejected.

Saul's power increased steadily. This is because it was redeemed by the Holy Spirit, and increased by the Holy Spirit's own power. Saul had *always* been powerful: now he was more so. And this power would continue to increase.

Saul's life teaches us about the power of the Spirit. When serving God correctly, Saul progressed rapidly. He matured visibly, his ministry was powerful and life-giving, his repentance bore remarkable fruit.

Several elements combined to produce Saul's maturity and power in service. He was obedient, doing exactly what God said. He prayed, and was open to what God revealed. He needed help from others, and accepted it from Ananias. He needed fellowship and the experience of others, and received it from the disciples in Damascus.

To grow in serving God we should be single-minded, obedient and prayerful. We must be wary of being isolated or independent. We need the help of others who serve God. This will keep us on the right track, going in the right direction.

Prayer

Father,
   I praise and thank you for the gift of the Holy Spirit.
   Send the Spirit anew into my life, to change, heal, restore. I want to be empowered to serve you more fully, to represent you more truly. By your Spirit lead me into your mysteries, free me to praise you. In Jesus' Name. Amen.

Practice

Ask the Lord to lead you to or put into your path, today or tomorrow, someone who needs your prayers. Pray with them.

Day 36

Saul Serves God with Boldness

---

*S*OME *time passed, and the Jews worked out a plot to kill him. But news of it reached Saul. They were keeping watch at the gates day and night in order to kill him, but the disciples took him by night and let him down from the wall, lowering him in a basket . . . When he reached Jerusalem . . . Saul started to go round with the disciples, preaching fearlessly in the name of the Lord. But after he had spoken to the Hellenists and argued with them, they became determined to kill him. When the brothers got to know of this, they took him to Caesarea and sent him off from there to Tarsus. (Acts 9:23–25; 29–30)*

If your life has ever been threatened, you know the depth of fear, the strength of terror that surges suddenly. Yet you don't have to have this awful experience to know what threat is: you're living in reaction to threat all the time.

Security is very important to us. Entire nations are preoccupied with it. The 'interests of national security' defend, justify and cover a multitude of sins.

Financial security is very important personally. Not just 'What shall we eat, what shall we drink, what shall we wear?', but much more broadly and deeply, 'What can we afford?' 'What assures our safety?' 'What pleasures our lives?'

Houses, mortgages, cars, furnishings, education, televisions, videos, tape recorders, motorbikes, boats, a second house, holidays – these are the material norms of our society. They set the standard for the world. So, increasingly, do security systems, guard dogs and personal weapons. We must protect our acquisitions. Investments, portfolios, property, speculation: all assure, as much as humanly possible, economic security. Those who still haven't food, who worry about the basics of life, are considered incompetent failures. They are discounted.

Job security is another worry. The unemployment rate jiggles up and down but doesn't basically change – nor will it, because technology has redefined the meaning of work and jobs. Education and qualifications don't necessarily secure anything. Age has become personal weakness – if one is 'too old', one risks the golden hand-shake or redundancy, displaced by re-organisation, replaced by 'software'.

Physical security is an escalating insecurity. More than half the women who live in London are afraid to go out alone at night. Mugging and rape are the twin terrors. The elderly are also frightened, hiding inside their homes because failing strength makes them incapable of defending themselves against attack. Children are increasingly at risk. Their trust and naivety, their dependence on adults, make them perfect victims for abuse and abduction.

The poor are insecure. Their lack of education or confidence often makes them unable to approach welfare centres to request even the small aid allotted.

In our times, people feel insecure. They spend time and money trying to protect themselves from danger, trying to preserve their lives and lifestyles.

Imagine then, the courage of someone who puts their life at risk deliberately.

Some people do it for money or thrill: working on oil rigs or pipe lines, living in hostile foreign countries, performing as tightrope walkers, animal keepers, test drivers, stuntspeople. Others risk danger for love or service. Missionaries do, some politicians and popes do, nuns and nursing sisters do.

Saul is in this latter group. For love of Christ, in

service to God, he risked death. And not just once, but time and again.

Once it got so bad that his friends had to smuggle him out of the city. Being packed in a basket and lowered over city walls in the dark of night would be more adventure and danger than some of us would ever look for. But to do it from *necessity*, under pain of death, is even more terrifying. If the rope broke, if someone didn't keep their weight steady, if the authorities had somehow been alerted and there were guards hidden below . . . these eventualities meant death. Certain death. Life stopped, taken away, finished. Not maybe, definitely.

Saul had alienated the authorities. Both church and state opposed him. He was a grave danger to the very hierarchy of which he had been the darling. There were no sentimental attachments preventing Saul's execution if he could be caught. He was a blasphemer and a powerful one, a preacher and an effective one, and a traitor as well.

Life is valuable and must be valued. Security is necessary, we weren't created to live in fear. But we must know what to fear and what to protect. Saul did. He knew exactly what he valued, what he would give his life to, what he would die for. It was the love of Christ, the service of God. For those, he would risk anything.

Are you the same? Is it because of loving Christ that you'd put yourself at risk? Is it because of serving God that authorities might seek you? Is the gospel of Jesus what you value most, what you give your time, money and energy to securing?

Prayer

Holy Spirit,
  It is by your presence, your purifying, that I feel safe in God. Have your way, Lord, in my heart, my life, my securities. Cleanse me from fear, strengthen me with

141

confidence, so I can trust God as much as I love him. I ask in Christ's Name. Amen.

Practice

With a friend, read Luke 12:16–21. Talk about it, working out the difference in your life between 'storing up treasure for yourself' and 'becoming rich in the sight of God.'

Day 37

Saul Serves God with Service to Others

---

*W*HILE *Barnabas and Saul were at Antioch some prophets came down from Jerusalem, and one of them whose name was Agabus, seized by the Spirit, stood up and predicted that a severe and universal famine was going to happen. This in fact happened while Claudius was emperor. The disciples decided to send relief, each to contribute what he could afford, to the brothers living in Judaea. They did this and delivered their contributions to the elders through the agency of Barnabas and Saul. (Acts 11:27–30)*

When was the last time you did something for someone? Something completely gratuitous, something completely unexpected. Not the last time you prepared a meal for those you love, or took food to the housebound or helped the young man in the office to look again at his career prospects. Not something you'd do normally, something that as friend, parent or mentor you'd be expected to do. When did you do something that was a pure gift of service on your part? Close your eyes and try to recall.

Can you think of anything? What prompted your action? Did you yourself recognise a need and determine to meet it, or did someone tell you?

In this story, Saul serves God by serving others. There were two needs, and Saul helped meet both. First, the fellowship at Jerusalem had to prepare for the famine. The concern and generosity of the Antioch community met this need. Then there was the second need, the delivery of their gift. Who would go? And the answer was, Barnabas and Saul.

This incident shows us many things about Saul's character. First, he was willing to go a *great* distance, by sea or land, to help others. He undertook discomfort and hardship to bear the gifts and greetings of the Antioch church, to help the church in Judea, to encourage those who would soon suffer. Saul spent his time, his energy and his life in practical service to others.

Second, Saul was flexible in how he served God. He wasn't a specialist, saying 'This isn't my ministry.' Saul's personal calling was greater than almost any other individual's in the early Christian world. Saul was essential to spreading God's salvation to pagans and Gentiles, Saul was unique in his gifts of learning, communication and intelligence. But he *never* set himself up as superior. He held back from no struggle, he never removed himself from the most basic, practical needs. Rather, he walked, rode, sailed, and ran, to carry out his mission. He worked, taught, travelled, settled, moved, to accomplish what God, the Holy Spirit and the early fellowships set before him. Saul was single-minded about his calling, and confident of his ministry: but he never used these certainties to avoid one sort of service and ensure another.

Thirdly, Saul was properly related to those in authority in both churches. It was a corporate decision to help the Jerusalem fellowship, and a corporate agreement that Barnabas and Saul should make the journey. Once arrived, their gift was delivered 'to the elders', and they decided what to do with it. Saul didn't make suggestions how to use it, he just gave it. There were no strings attached and Saul didn't weave any of his own.

Paul supported good order, not personal gain. He didn't use his job as agent to become manager, as emissary to become organiser. Although gifted, powerful and famous, in this instance Saul was merely a servant, one carrying love and practical relief. A servant he remained.

Think again about your recent, freely offered service.

Are there similarities between you and Saul? Were you merely God's agent? Or, if roundly congratulated or soundly thanked, were you flattered? Was your service something you'd normally do, or was it unusual for you, requiring effort in a truly sacrificial way? Was your service really generous or did it reward your sense of self-worth, gratifying a hidden pocket of self-seeking?

Did your action support, bear and encourage, as Saul's did? Were you submitted to those in charge: hospital sisters, organisers of the relief charity, relatives of the needy? Or were you so sure of the value of what you were doing or giving that you felt these others needed to be put straight in some way, that they didn't actually have the proper understanding?

Don't be afraid to examine closely both what you did and why you did it. If you discover unpleasant truths about your seemingly altruistic service, God will help you face them and learn from them.

What if you couldn't recall any extraordinary service you'd undertaken? Perhaps you're unsure what your gifts are anyway, uncertain about your ordinary service. If so, begin to pray that God will show you, directly or through others, the gifts you have and the particular calling God has for you. Pray not just once or twice, but frequently. Pursue God, so you'll have the pleasure and confidence of knowing personally that he has called you.

Talk to others, too, those you respect and admire. Find out how they have got where they are in their service to God. Also ask them what they think about you, and your possible ministries.

As an overall guideline, obey Saul, who says, 'In the service of the Lord, work not half-heartedly but with conscientiousness and an eager spirit. Be joyful in hope, persevere in hardship; keep praying regularly, share with any of God's holy people who are in need; look for opportunities to be hospitable.' (Ro. 12:11–13)

Prayer

Lord Jesus,

From Saul's life I see how powerful the gift of serving can be. I pray that I will serve whole-heartedly and well. I pray that in things large and small my life will witness to your love and testify to the truth. Amen.

Practice

If you haven't performed a special service recently, think of one now. Do it sometime in the next two days. If you have, perform another. Do it within the next two days. Don't tell anyone about it.

Day 38

Saul Serves God with Preparation

---

*I*N *the church at Antioch the following were prophets
and teachers: Barnabas, Simeon called Niger, Lucius
of Cyrene, Manaen, who had been brought up with Herod
the tetrarch, and Saul. One day while they were offering
worship to the Lord and keeping a fast, the Holy Spirit
said, 'I want Barnabas and Saul set apart for the work
to which I have called them.' So it was that after fasting
and prayer they laid their hands on them and sent them
off. (Acts 13:1–3)*

'In the beginning, God.' This is how our history begins.
It's how our perception of God and God's relationship
to creation is first grasped. 'In the beginning, God.'

In the beginning God knew, God loved, God spoke,
God made. In the beginning God intended: and brought
into being that which was envisioned. 'In the beginning,
God.'

In each of our beginnings, God also knew, loved,
created. Our personalities, our gifts, our abilities, capa-
bilities, disabilities: God has known from the beginning.
Our lives, our desires, our loves, our needs: God knew
from the beginning. The unique calling each of us has,
the particular service we can render to God, the meaning
of our individual lives, whatever our capacities or depri-
vations, whatever our true or false ambitions or images:
God knows.

This knowledge is beyond us. We can accept it only
by faith, we can believe it only by hope, we can trust
it only by love. Our understanding is too limited to
comprehend it. How can God know but not control,

perceive but not predestine? How can God compel us in perfect freedom?

In speaking to Ananias, God revealed that he knew Saul's exact place in his plan. 'This man is my chosen instrument to bring my name before Gentiles and kings and before the people of Israel.' And later, Saul himself testifies to his experience of calling: 'God, who had set me apart from the time when I was in my mother's womb, called me through his grace and chose to reveal his son in me, so that I should preach him to the Gentiles.' (Gal. 1:15–16)

But Saul, before entering fully into this mission which had been his since conception, had much to learn. For a time he was with Christian fellowships in Damascus, Jerusalem and Tarsus; he left each place under threat of death because of the power of his preaching and the upheaval it caused. Finally he escaped into Arabia, where he lived for several years, hiding from King Aretas and apparently without Christian fellowship or support. These were quiet years, spent in prayer, getting to know God better, reconciling his past with his present, his previous Pharisaical life with his current Christian commitment. Then back to activity and fellowship, in Antioch and Jerusalem.

Consider the elements which shaped Paul's ability to fulfill his service to God. There was shared life, worship and fellowship with other Christians. There was personal prayer, and long hours with God. There was teaching, as he learned from those more mature in Christ, as he gave them the benefits of his knowledge. There was travel, for mission and ministry, there was danger, stress and privation, enduring persecution, slipping through the clutches of death.

There was the challenge of making and maintaining relationships: loving and serving practically, getting along with others consistently, sharing the work of God. There was the need to become stabilised, to strengthen those resources the future would demand.

It often takes God years to prepare people for their ministry. Jesus lived for thirty years at Nazareth, being a reliable son, learning a trade, working in the family business, going to services regularly, being disciplined by prayer, the scriptures, his relationships with God, family, friends and villagers.

Mother Teresa, an outstanding servant of Christ, also spent years being prepared for her vocation of serving 'the poorest of the poor.'

It was twenty years from the time she entered her order to the time she went out to establish a work of mercy. For years she was disciplined by convent life, learning personal responsibility, group commitment, spiritual integrity. She spent years in prayer, worshipping, adoring, labouring. She worked in education for nearly two decades, first as a teacher, then as a principal. She acquired the techniques of teaching and experienced its demanding monotony. She shouldered the responsibilities and frustrations of administration. She became skilled in the diplomacy and firmness required by a head mistress. Only after all this preparation did she go forth, to found the work which has made her famous.

God will either train us himself, as with Jesus, Saul and Mother Teresa, or will use all that life has given and required of us, to perfect us as servants. God knows the calling for each of us: God's desire is that we know it too. If we respond obediently God will elaborate, refine, make clearer, how we take up that calling; and, in the fullness of time, we will enter into it completely, as did Jesus, Saul, Mother Teresa.

Nothing in life is beyond God's redemption, nothing will be lost. There is no work, no activity, no experience, that God cannot make new, and use for his glory. If our hearts are set to serve God, God will give us our heart's desire. Paul declares, 'We are well aware that God works with those who love him, those who have been called in accordance with his purpose, and turns everything to their good.' (Ro. 8:29)

Just so. God is able to accomplish all he desires. 'In the beginning, God.'

Prayer

Holy Spirit,

Silence my clamour, still my soul. Settle my uncertainties, so I will know that you lead me. Confirm my calling in Christ, to love, to serve, to care. Do all that will help me to serve more faithfully, enable me to understand how God sees my life, and to see with his sight. Guide me and prepare me, for now and the future. Amen.

Practice

Ask a friend to recommend a short biography, in words or pictures, of someone whose service to God has touched them.

Day 39

Saul Serves God with Discernment

---

*A*T *Paphos the proconsul summoned Barnabas and
Saul and asked to hear the word of God. But Elymas
the Jewish magician and false prophet tried to stop them so
as to prevent the proconsul's conversion to the faith.*

*Then Saul, whose other name is Paul, filled with the
Holy Spirit, looked at him intently and said, 'You utter
fraud, you impostor, you son of the devil, you enemy of all
uprightness, will you not stop twisting the straightforward
ways of the Lord? Now watch how the hand of the Lord
will strike you: you will be blind, and for a time you will
not see the sun.' That instant, everything went misty and
dark for him, and he groped about to find someone to lead
him by the hand.*

*Then the proconsul, who had watched everything,
became a believer, being much struck by what he had
learnt about the Lord. (Acts 13:7–12)*

It will not do to deny that evil is real and powerful.
We can philosophise about it, intellectualise it or be
embarrassed by it: all to our detriment.

The world is spiritual first and material second: we
are deceived if we think that what we see, touch, taste
and smell is the prime reality. We are foolish if we think
that murder and rape, greed and corruption, dismember-
ment and torture, are without spiritual roots. They *are*
the fruit of broken lives, broken families, of minds and
feelings poisoned by deception and crazed by deprivation: but all this brokeness, deception and deprivation
has other roots than just the physical, the material, the
emotional. Paul warns Christians 'It is not against human

enemies that we have to struggle, but against the princi-
palities and the ruling forces who are masters of the
darkness in this world, the spirits of evil in the heavens.'
(Eph. 6:12)

Jesus was also emphatic about the reality of evil. 'The
devil was a murderer from the start; he was never
grounded in the truth; there is no truth in him at all.
When he lies he is speaking true to his nature, because
he is a liar, and the father of lies.' (John 8:44b)

The truth of Jesus' words are seen here irrefutably.
Filled with the Holy Spirit, Saul was empowered by
God to recognise spiritual truth and thereby spiritual
deception.

The names Saul uses are significant. Elymas the false
prophet is called *fraud* and *impostor*. Both these words
define someone who lies, who deceives, who uses circumstances and evidence to trick.

Saul links this deceit with Satan, calling the magician
son of the devil, enemy of uprightness. This deception for
evil gain and personal power is related to the devil, who
always tries to prevent the truth of God's love and saving
grace from being known.

Saul next attacks the subtlety of false argument. '*The
Lord's ways*', he declares, '*are straightforward: stop
twisting them!*' Causing confusion is another of the devil's
works, because it prevents the *simple* truth of God's
loving purposes being heard or believed.

Saul next proclaims the power of God to cripple and
undo the power of evil. Elymas was a magician, skilled
in the black arts: now he will be the victim of his own
works of darkness. He'll stumble in the panic of blindness, the mist of uncertainty, the blackness of life
without the sun.

For Elymas himself had rejected the Son. He saw the
shining light of Christ and preferred the devil's darkness.
But that darkness vanished in God's light.

Elymas himself was deceived. As a magician, he had
thought himself powerful and invulnerable. Now he

found himself powerless and dependent. He *groped about to find someone to lead him by the hand*. The devil had tricked his servant: Elymas had no real power to withstand the Holy Spirit's power.

God will not be mocked. God will train his servants to distinguish between good and evil, light and dark. If we are committed to serving God, to 'working the works of righteousness', God gives us all the power of heaven to name and to put in order the things of earth which are darkened and deceived.

Notice that Saul was not overly excited. He wasn't histrionic or loud. He merely *looked at him intently*, then spoke. The power of speaking God's truth carried its own weight.

Nor was Saul alone. He had a companion in the faith, Barnabas, an experienced and mature Christian.

Nor did Saul perform any great actions. He simply looked, saw, spoke. God by the Holy Spirit did all the rest.

As partakers of Christ, members of Christ's body on earth, we are to do the works of Christ. Let us offer ourselves and our service to God, that we may be matured, discerning, faithful, obedient. Let us learn to recognise and name the fraudulent works of evil, let us exercise God's authority intently, calmly, certainly. Let us learn from Saul, from Barnabas, from the Holy Spirit. Then others will be like the proconsul, who *became a believer, being much struck by what he had learnt about the Lord.*

Prayer

Pure light of the Son of God,
  Shine on my path, that I may see the way you have
    called me to go.
Shine on my path, that I may follow you.
Pure love of the Son of God,
  Fill my heart, that I may show the love you have for
    all mankind,

love that is eternal life.
Spirit of the Son of God,
    Live in me, that I may do the will of God and be set
      free to live
the life of Jesus Christ. Amen. (Mimi Farra)

Practice

Talk through today's scripture and meditation with some
friends.

Day 40

Saul Serves God with Vision

SAUL and his companions went by sea from Paphos to Perga in Pamphylia where John left them to go back to Jerusalem. The others carried on from Perga till they reached Antioch in Pisidia. (Acts 13:13–14)

It didn't take Saul long to join the great tradition of pilgrimage which is a sign of the Spirit's work. Jesus said, 'The Spirit blows where it will', and Saul, faithful to God, followed.

Already he's gone up and down Israel several times, crossed the sea to Cyprus, gone north to Pamphylia and Pisidia. All in just the first few years of his travelling ministry.

Saul loved God more than anyone or anything else in the world. Saul wanted, more than anything else in the world, to serve God. To serve God whole-heartedly and well. And he did.

Saul was willing to go anywhere, do anything, encounter anyone, to proclaim the wonderful news of God's salvation. Saul was willing to travel anywhere, settle anywhere, work anywhere, to announce the good news of Jesus Christ. Saul ate or fasted, drank or thirsted, stayed or went, was free or imprisoned, to witness to the resurrection of Christ. He did anything and everything the Spirit indicated.

The Holy Spirit is the leader of the pilgrimage to which God calls those who will serve. It was the way of the Spirit Saul and the other Christians sought, it was the Spirit they heard. The Spirit led, opened, closed; the Spirit moved, halted, spoke.

The Spirit called Saul to travel far and wide, back and forth, up and down, revealing God to those with no history or knowledge of God. Pagans and Gentiles were now, by the work of Christ, being joined to God. It was no longer only the Jews who could experience the height and depth of God's love: it was, after thousands of years of outworking, since the time of Adam, Noah and Abram, *all* people.

Saul helped God fulfill his promise to Abram: 'I shall make you a great nation, I shall bless you and make your name famous; you are to be a blessing! . . . all clans on earth will bless themselves by you. All nations on earth will bless themselves by your descendants, because you have obeyed my command.' (Genesis 12:2, 3b; 22:18) Without Saul, this would *not* have happened.

It's unnerving to see how committed God is to his work of salvation. Generation after generation, God instigates change, sends renewal, challenges assumptions, to accomplish what he intends. Generation after generation, God refuses to be limited, held behind the barriers of distance, culture or tradition. He sends those he has called far and wide to share his love and proclaim his word.

Many of God's people in our age are mobile, as Saul was. They travel from Africa to Australia, from London to Latin America, from America to Europe, in obedience to God's Spirit. They preach and teach, witnessing to the works of God: the salvation of Christ, the healing and restoring power of the Spirit, the call to fellowship, community and shared life.

Sometimes, as with Saul, God asks us to reduce and relocate. We are to sell or give away most of our possessions and move to another land to serve God. Frequently it is whole families or groups that are called, not just individuals.

Other times God asks us to remain where we are, but live a pilgrim life anyway. We are not to accumulate possessions which then distract. We are not to be hindered by investments and securities that tie our souls to the world. We are to stay flexible, able to respond obediently to a word of change from the Spirit.

This is because God's plan of salvation is universal. The work of God through Christ on the Cross and now by the Spirit is to be shared, proclaimed and demonstrated. But since God is personal, he'll almost always use people to preach, teach and witness. So as God's servants we must be like Saul, with a big heart able to respond to a big vision, and as little as possible to encumber us. We must be capable of hearing a universal word, one for all people, all nations, all cultures. We mustn't limit God by our limitations, prevent God's intents by our parochialism or materialism.

As Jesus said to his disciples, 'Whoever serves me, must follow me, and my servant will be with me wherever I am.' (John 12:26) Jesus is led by the Spirit, obeying the will of God. If we want to be with him, we must go where he goes. Saul always did.

Prayer

Dear Lord,

In your service I want to find perfect freedom. I love your word, although I don't always understand or appreciate your ways.

Renew my desire to follow you, perfect my ability to serve you. Send again your Spirit, to broaden my vision. I long to be with you, near you, like you. I pray in your Name, Jesus. Amen.

Practice

Discuss with family or friends the likelihood of being able to re-locate, should God ask you to. Is it 'impossible'?

Other Marshall Pickering Paperbacks

THROUGH DAVID'S PSALMS

Derek Prince

Derek Prince, internationally known Bible teacher and scholar, draws on his understanding of the Hebrew language and culture, and a comprehensive knowledge of Scripture, to present 101 meditations from the Psalms.

Each of these practical and enriching meditations is based on a specific passage and concludes with a faith response. They can be used either for personal meditation or for family devotions. They are intended for all those who want their lives enriched or who seek comfort and encouragement from the Scriptures.

LOVING GOD

Charles Colson

Loving God is the very purpose of the believer's life, the vocation for which he is made. However loving God is not easy and most people have given little real thought to what the greatest commandment really means.

Many books have been written on the individual subjects of repentence, Bible study, prayer, outreach, evangelism, holiness and other elements of the Christian life. In **Loving God**, Charles Colson draws all these elements together to look at the entire process of growing up as a Christian.

Combining vivid illustrations with straightforward exposition he shows how to live out the Christian faith in our daily lives. **Loving God** provides a real challenge to deeper commitment and points the way towards greater maturity.

OUT OF THE MELTING POT

Bob Gordon

Faith does not operate in a vacuum, it operates in human lives. God wants your life to be a crucible of faith.
Bob Gordon draws together Biblical principles and personal experience to provide valuable insights into this key area. Particular reference is made to the lessons he leant recently as God provided £600,000 to buy Roffey Place Christian Training Centre.
Out of the Melting Pot is Bob Gordon's powerful testimony to the work of God today and a profound challenge to shallow views of faith.

BILLY GRAHAM

John Pollock

By any reckoning, Billy Graham is one of the major religious figures of the twentieth-century.
John Pollock tells the highlights of the Billy Graham story briefly and vividly for the general reader. Using existing material and brand new information the story is taken right up the eve of Mission England.
This is an authoritative biography which pays special attention to the recent developments in Dr. Graham's life and ministry. Fully endorsed by Billy Graham himself, the book is full of fascinating new insights into the man and his mission.

". . . fascinating reading"
London Bible College Review
". . . a difficult book to put down"
Church of England Newspaper

DATE DUE

P.S. If you have ideas for new Christian Books or other products, please write to us too!